To my precious ▮▮▮▮▮▮▮▮▮ *hel*

Love, Mom

DAUGHTERS OF EVE
DAUGHTERS OF GOD

April, 2008

Lets strive together and help one another be Daughters of God.

Brenda Weaver

Christian Light Publications, Inc.
Harrisonburg, Virginia 22802

DAUGHTERS OF EVE, DAUGHTERS OF GOD

Christian Light Publications, Inc.,
Harrisonburg, Virginia 22802
© 2007 by Christian Light Publications, Inc.
All rights reserved. Published 2007
Printed in the United States of America

Cover photos: © iStockphoto.com and
              © Christian Light Publications

Cover design: Jotham Yoder

ISBN: 978-0-87813-646-9

Dedicated to:

My daughters, LaNell, Lori, and Holly
who listened to sentences and paragraphs,
helped me navigate the computer,
and washed lots of laundry and dishes while I wrote.
I thrill to see you mature as daughters of God.

To my mother, Evelyn (Gehman, Furtak) Groff,
with gratitude for your mothering,
and deep appreciation for your faith.
Thank you for blessing this writing
with your affirmation.

In memory of my father, Joseph Furtak,
the son of a Polish immigrant and the object of my
daughterly affections.
You taught me much more than you realized.
Thank you.

To my husband, John,
whose gift of a briefcase and an updated computer
told me he believed I could do this work.
Thank you for trusting me and allowing me to write
the message the Lord laid on my heart.

Acknowledgements:

Thank you to:

- God, who fills me with joy in believing.

- Friends who critiqued my work and encouraged me to continue: Evelyn Landes, Clara Swartzentruber, Janice Shively, Judy Yoder, Tracy Burkholder, Deb Snare, Michelle Beidler, and my Writer's Circle friends.

- Christian Light Publications, their editors, evaluators, and everyone who assists with their annual writers' conferences.

- Ralph and Evelyn Landes who graciously and cheerfully hosted me for all those conferences.

- Our ministry team at Millmont Mennonite Church for teaching me so much and for faithfully preaching the Word of God.

- Editors Fred Miller and Leon Yoder for their patience and kindness in editing, and their confidence that readers were waiting for this message of hope.

Contents

Preface

"For as the heaven is high above the earth,
so great is his mercy toward them that fear him.
As far as the east is from the west, so far hath
he removed our transgressions from us.
Like as a father pitieth his children,
so the LORD *pitieth them that fear him.*
For he knoweth our frame;
he remembereth that we are dust."
Psalm 103:11-14

How comforting to know that our heavenly Father remembers that we are created of dust. We are daughters of Eve. Amazingly, in our weakness, God invites us to be His very own—daughters of God. Sometimes we fail to realize the wonder of that royal invitation. Living victoriously as daughters of God continues to be a daily challenge, because we are still very much daughters of Eve.

If only my circumstances were different . . . We tend to groan about and react to what we have been given or not given. Allowing God to use those very circumstances as instruments to refine us brings peace.

Parts of my personal story appear in this book, not because I readily accepted my circumstances but because God lovingly taught me to embrace them and yield to His powerful redemptive work. The things that had angered me, the conditions that had profoundly affected me, were actually gifts entrusted to me by a loving God so that I can live to the glory of His grace. As a five-year-old fearfully watching our family break apart, I could not comprehend how God would fill the empty longings of an aching daughter's heart. When I turned twenty our family was reunited physically, but God was not finished working in our hearts. Now, at forty-five, I look back on a life full of God's forgiveness and grace.

When I look ahead I see shadows of fear lurking on my journey of life. But I know God can do amazing things. I know He loves me and that the circumstances I may experience are tools He uses to transform this dusty daughter of Eve into a crowned daughter of God.

As you read, you will identify with struggles and strengths that are common to daughters of Eve. I pray you will thrill at the joy of living in victory as daughters of God.

In several of the accounts included in this book, names and details were changed to protect the identity of the people who shared their thoughts or stories and wished to remain anonymous.

His daughter,

Brenda Weaver

WE ARE
DAUGHTERS

CHAPTER 1

Daughters Indeed

*F*aded maroon and gray, the old, flannel housecoat holds just a hint of a familiar smell. Occasionally I dust it off, straighten the belt, and give it a quick hug before I tuck it away in the back of my closet. A visit with my peculiar treasure always beckons me back.

I pause to view my six-year-old reflection in the mirror before I tug on the wardrobe door. I listen. Has anyone heard the creak of the door, evidence of my exploring? The smell of cedar envelopes me as I leaf through the articles of clothing that hang side by side like the pages of a large mysterious book.

First is the sailor's uniform—a navy, hazy shadow under plastic. A yellowed wedding dress peers through layers of tissue paper. I stretch to reach the bag dangling from the next hanger. The baby's green hat and sweater is so small; did I really wear it? Next come several coats that sleepily wait for winter; the neck of one is circled with soft fur. From there my hand easily glides to the soft gray and maroon housecoat—a man's housecoat— worn and faded, but not tattered or unusable.

As that six-year-old youngster, I knew part of the story. The lanky, teenage sailor had outgrown the scratchy wool suit before he married Mother. Each of us children had worn the green sweater and cap. Coats could be used another season. But the housecoat . . . why was it here? Why was it empty? What was the man really like who had worn it? Why had his fist pounded the supper table so often? Would he come back?

I did not know it then, but that empty housecoat held more than just pain and longing; it held a gift for me. The gift was invisible at first. When I grew older I recognized it, but I certainly did not consider it a gift. Now I cannot bring myself to throw the worn, old housecoat away. I loved the man who wore it; I longed for the man who left it; and I have come to embrace the gift that lay hidden in its empty folds.

Even after I recognized the gift, I had a lot to learn about the Giver. Some people told me God didn't really *give* the gift, but I knew He had allowed it to be given to me. Some people said it wasn't a *gift*, and I should not thank God for sin; I came to understand that I could thank Him for choosing me to be born into circumstances that resulted from sin but revealed God's grace. Some people said to *forget* the gift and get on with the really important things in life; I saw that the gift was an integral part of my journey, holding messages and miracles that were too important to forget.

I can tell you about the housecoat. I can still show it to you. But the lessons I learned and the gift I came to recognize are part of my journey as a daughter — a daughter of Eve and a daughter of God.

Daughters Indeed

Each of us is born of someone, so all women are daughters, clear back to Adam and Eve. You may have misgivings, as I did, about being a daughter, or you may have confidence in being a daughter. You may even have been rejected, neglected, or disrespected. Whatever your earthly journey as a daughter entails, God offers you a unique daughterhood. Born as daughters of Eve, we inherited her humanity and we share in bearing the image of God (Genesis 1:26, 27). We are invited to be adopted as daughters of God (Ephesians 1:5). Through salvation we receive the Holy Spirit (1 Corinthians 12:13). One day believers will be united with Christ as part of His bride. A beautiful, three-part daughterhood awaits. We can be God's daughters by creation (daughters of Eve), daughters by adoption (daughters of God), and daughters-in-law by union with God's Son (daughters for eternity). Just think of it! Let your thoughts peer into the wonder of the invitation.

You and I are daughters of Eve, invited to journey forward as daughters of God. We are fragile at times, fallible, and femininely human. But the Lord's glory is manifested as we submit to being chastened, cherished, and challenged onward as daughters of God. Oh, it is a journey, and journeys vary from one individual to another; but God's grace is sufficient for each one. A garland of grace, eternity in heaven, an intimate relationship with God the Father as part of the bride of Christ — the rewards outweigh the struggle by far!

Gifts

God's gifts to daughters also include individualized personality traits, temperament, heritage, and family. Nor did we at birth choose our community, environment, or country. These things were inherited from our parents' genes or determined by their decisions. The fact that you and I received them is a gift of God's providence.

What about the circumstances and experiences of our lives — including those that trouble us? "Now wait just a minute. Are we going to call our circumstances a gift from God?" you may ask incredulously. Or you may say: "Don't blame God for my experiences; they were the result of sinful decisions." God may not have *caused* your circumstances, and some experiences do result from sin, but God *did allow* them. (Dare we entertain the thought that anything is beyond His control?) God allows us choices, and then He uses them for His honor and glory. I suggest that within our circumstances and experiences are gifts such as pain or empty longings. They are gifts because they call us to meet God.

"Where is God?" Job asked. "Oh that one would hear me! behold, my desire is, that the Almighty would answer me." (Job 31:35). Job's experiences drove him to seek audience with God. God replied to Job's questions with more than seventy questions of His own. When the soul-searching had concluded, Job knew a lot more about himself (how little he had known) and a lot more about God (what an awesome, sovereign Giver He is).

What gifts have you been given? Shattered dreams? Unfulfilled longings? A faithful family? A family that mocks your faith? The loss of a parent, spouse, or child? A godly heritage? A church that practices Bible principles? Some are easily recognized as gifts; some are wrapped thickly in grief and pain so that only honest seekers find the less-than-obvious bequest. God can use whatever you or I have been given to show us Himself.

Under the Circumstances

Although our youngest daughter is approaching adolescence, she loves to be tucked into bed each evening. If my husband tucks her in, I am sure to hear peels of childish laughter delightfully mixed with deep bass chuckles. Sometimes both of us tuck her in, much to her delight. Our hearts are warmed by her sincere thanks and appeals to God. (Her prayers are more insightful than one which her older sibling had uttered as a preschooler: "Lord, please help the heifers to become Christians." Apparently he thought that would change the behavior of the ornery ones he had watched his father chase back inside the fence!)

When I tuck our daughter into bed, our conversation often goes like this:

"I'm so glad you are my mother." Her arms slip around my neck.

"And I am so glad you are my daughter." I return her squeeze.

Last night when I tucked her in, tears coursed down her red-blotched cheeks. "I am so glad you and Dad are Christians, and that we do not have war here." I knew the tears were born out of her compassionate, sensitive spirit. Before going to bed she had read a personal account written by a boy her age. In the mission newsletter, he had described how he had watched rebels torture and kill his father and mother. How terrifying for that young boy. Just reading about it from far away was frightening enough for my own child. What promises could I offer her? That war will never come to our small town? That God would never let anything like that happen to her? To not worry, that her dad and I would not be killed by rebels?

I could not truthfully promise her any of these things. While it is unlikely she will witness something so horrifying, I cannot promise her that I can — or that God will — spare her from horrendous testing and trial. I cannot promise her that as her parents we will always be there for her. In fact, because we are human and sinful, we will at times fail. I can (and did) show her from the Scripture that God will never leave or forsake her. I can convey an important message to her: God is our Father and He will not allow anything to happen to us that His grace will not enable us to bear.

That consolation comforted my daughter as she drifted off to sleep. After challenging the rest of the family, the newsletter was tossed away. But what about the young child who experienced the horror? Memories are not easily tossed into a wastebasket. God's nearness is not readily felt by one who feels so forsaken.

I dug the newsletter out of the wastebasket. *What were the child's last words?* "God bless the Christian Aid Ministries sponsors."[1] *Amazing. A child who lost so much, who waits in an orphanage for food and someone to care for him — this child asks God to bless me?*

What had this child done with his emptiness and need? He longed for and received help. He praised God and blessed his helpers. His great need was a "gift" that drove him to look for help.

I am compelled to search my soul. *What have I done with the emptiness I found in a closeted housecoat? How have I channeled that longing? What am I doing with the help I have received? What other circumstances in my life — be they filled with pain or joy — is God working together for my good? Am I using them for His glory?*

Do you need to ask yourself similar questions? What have you done with the joys and disappointments of life? Have you received them? Have you recognized the gifts that are hidden there? Have you allowed the circumstances of your life to call you close to God in your journey as His daughter?

When Jesus Tarries

As Jesus tarried on the dusty road to Bethany, questions tugged at the hearts of two daughters of Eve: "Lord, if thou hadst been here, my brother had not died" (John 11:21, 32). Jesus countered their limited faith with the hope of resurrection and life. He was deeply moved by the grief of these weeping sisters, and He wept with them at the grave of their brother Lazarus. Why would the Saviour cry when He planned to soon raise the dead man? He cried in empathy with His friends, but I believe He also shed tears over their lack of faith. Even when Jesus commanded that the stone be taken away from the cave where Lazarus lay, Martha protested. His words to her pulsate with meaning at whatever death-filled, covered cave we may face: "Said I not unto thee, that, if thou wouldest believe, thou shouldest see the glory of God?" (John 11:40). When Lazarus breathed again, God's glory bounded from the walls of that cave, and belief shone in the hearts of the sisters and many of the mourners. The grief-filled circumstances Mary and Martha faced were a "gift" that enabled them to see the glory of God.

Accept the Gifts

The Lord still yearns for daughters of Eve facing difficult circumstances. He prays for us (Romans 8:27). And He knows if we believe, as daughters of God, we will see the glory of God. "For I reckon that the sufferings of this present time are not worthy to be compared with the glory which shall be revealed in us" (Romans 8:18).

Do not refuse the gifts God has given you. Years may pass before we recognize our severest trials as gifts, but God's grace is abundant. His glory will be evident when we allow the stones to be rolled away from caves of grief and emptiness. The circumstances and experiences of life are tools in God's hand to move us forward on our journeys as daughters of God. Sometimes He chastises. Sometimes He challenges. Always He shows us His cherishing love.

Journey of a Daughter

Remember the feeling of rapture and delight when you were adopted as a daughter of God? Your familiar old world wore a new look, and your heart overflowed with love. Deep, abiding peace wrapped itself around your soul like a cozy blanket placed over your shivering shoulders by a loving parent. A light began to shine in your heart like the soft glow of a night-light in the threatening darkness. You wanted always to experience that peace, protection, and the squeaky-clean feeling of having your sins forgiven. Do you also remember how soon you faced the fact that you were still very much a daughter of Eve? Those first unkind words that wounded a friend? That lie that pricked your conscience until you confessed? A struggle with impure thoughts?

We realized quickly that our conversion did not automatically eliminate all natural human behavior. Then we began the lifelong lesson of what it means to die to self and live transformed as a daughter of God. The Apostle Paul said, "For the good that I would I do not: but the evil which I would not, that I do" (Romans 7:19). This mighty man of God was well aware of the struggle of our two natures, the old and the new; he also knew that by the grace of God we can put off the old man and put on the new. Valiantly, he pressed on, as should we. He also penned Romans 8, a chapter rich with the transforming power of a sovereign God. "But if the Spirit of him that raised up Jesus from the dead dwell in you, he that raised up Christ from the dead shall also quicken your mortal bodies by his Spirit that dwelleth in you" (Romans 8:11). Yes, we can be "more than conquerors through him that loved us" (verse 37).

Paralyzed Potential?

The devil knows the power and positive effect of a transformed life. He wishes to paralyze our potential and render us powerless to advance the kingdom of our adoptive Father. He likes nothing better than to see us lulled by our limitations, frozen by fear, paralyzed by powerlessness, defective by denial, or encumbered by cares (which may be his favorite). And so he whispers lies to us:

"God cannot fill your emptiness. He cannot heal your wounds." (Then the devil offers a variety of cheap, ineffective fillers and salves that he claims will fill and heal.)

"If you still do that, you must not be a child of God." (Dished out with discouragement.)

"You can't witness for Christ; you will fail." (And the fear of man overpowers one's fear of God.)

"Don't try to serve God in that way or in that place; you will suffer for it." "You failed again; you won't ever be able to overcome that habit." (While attacking your good intentions.)

"You can't be an effective Christian . . . have you forgotten your past?" (While he riddles us with thoughts of self-condemnation.)

"You are too busy to have your quiet time with God today." (Another favorite of the devil's.)

From the time the fire of God's love begins to flicker

in your heart, the devil tries to douse it. He wants to extinguish the warm night-light of hope.

Fanning Into Flame

As surely as the devil wishes to douse that flickering spark, God wishes to fan it into flame. "For thou wilt light my candle: the LORD my God will enlighten my darkness. For by thee I have run through a troop; and by my God have I leaped over a wall" (Psalm 18:28, 29). Troops to run through, walls to leap over, wounds to heal, emptiness to fill—whatever the trials of life, God's strength is readily available to daughters of God. He has enlightened our darkness. He expects us to reflect that light. "Let your light so shine before men, that they may see your good works, and glorify your Father which is in heaven" (Matthew 5:16).

What circumstances or experiences is God using in your life to fan the fire He ignited when you became a daughter of God? Or is He fanning away the chaff that lingers—the parts of your daughter of Eve that need to be burned?

Hidden in a Housecoat

For me the cavities of an empty housecoat held the gift of a longing to know. What began as a longing to really know my earthly father was transformed into an intense desire to know my heavenly Father. Yes, the pain was a gift. Step by step I have become more aware of the reality of being a daughter of Eve and the wonder of being a daughter of God!

As I finish rewriting Chapter 1, I am snuggling a premature infant against my heart. Tears slide down my cheek as her tiny fingers wrap around one of my own. While I care for this tiny baby, her family is attending her mother's funeral. Cancer claimed the life of the young mother just one day before baby Sharon was welcomed home from the hospital by her grieving father and siblings. Her mother, Grace, is gone from this life, but another grace has come to comfort and strengthen this family.

Someday this child may finger an empty housecoat and feel a longing to know. When she does, God will be there, confirming her birth as a daughter of Eve and inviting her to become a cherished daughter of God.

Whatever your circumstances, you are invited too.

Scriptures

Suggested Reading: Romans 8

"For as many as are led by the Spirit of God,
they are the sons of God.
For ye have not received the spirit of bondage again
to fear; But ye have received the Spirit of adoption,
whereby we cry, Abba, Father.
The Spirit itself beareth witness with our spirit,
that we are the children of God:
And if children, then heirs; heirs of God,
and joint-heirs with Christ;
if so be that we suffer with him, that we
may be also glorified together."
Romans 8:14-17

"The LORD is good, a strong hold in the day of trouble; and he knoweth [cherishes[2]] them that trust in him." Nahum 1:7

11

Prayer

Dear God,

I am a woman, a daughter of Eve. You remember that I am but dust (Psalm 103:14). You created me and You are completely familiar with my humanity. Your own Son became human.

I am amazed that even in my frailty You want to adopt me as a daughter of Your very own. I could never earn such a matchless gift. Your Word says: "For by grace are ye saved through faith; and that not of yourselves: it is the gift of God: Not of works, lest any man should boast. For we are his workmanship." (Ephesians 2:8-10). Thank You for Your gift of salvation. May I walk worthy of the vocation to which I am called (Ephesians 4:1).

Thank You for continuing to work on me through various gifts You have given me, even the circumstances and experiences that trouble me. You love me more than any earthly parent could, and You are committed to helping me live victoriously as a daughter of God. May I submit to Your chastisement and the challenges You present so that I may become more Christlike: an instrument for Your kingdom, a cherished daughter for Your glory, part of the bride of Christ.

Your Daughter,

_____

CHAPTER 2

Lord, let us be—

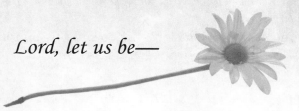

Daughters of Purpose

A simple song drifted over my dew-wet garden. I stilled my hoe. Glancing skyward I saw an eastern phoebe glide toward the branches of our maple tree. Her small chest swelled as she perched there. "Fee-bee, fee-bee, fee-bee." Her simple song matched her appearance—nothing remarkable. No brightly colored feathers. No ruby throat or pink-hued breast. Yet she shared her song so readily, as if she were unaware of her lack of luster. A sudden breeze crested her head feathers into a quaint cap. Her simplicity was attractive. Oblivious to how I scrutinized her olive-brown form, the phoebe darted to another branch and called again.

A call echoed within my heart, "Daugh-ter, Daughter . . ." *Yes, God, I'm listening. I have not forgotten. What do You want me to do? Share things I've learned on my journey as Your daughter? But God . . .* With trepidation I laid down my hoe and picked up my pen while I whispered a prayer. *God, if a simple phoebe can sing so readily, I will risk sharing my story to praise the glory of Your grace.* And so began this written journey, drawn from my personal journey as a daughter of Eve and a daughter of God.

Every daughter of God has a testimony regarding the

13

difference God's grace has made in her life. We may hesitate to share it with others, but God's call is unwavering: *use the circumstances I have allowed in your life to live for My glory.*

Join me in answering God's call to sing—in simplicity, in sincerity, with purpose, and in truth.

In Simplicity

No fine feathers, not even wing bars or eye-rings, distinguish the phoebe as she perches perkily on a wire. Her tail pumps up and down, as if to provide balance or incite action. Quickly she darts after an insect, finds a new perch, and resumes repeating her name: "Fee-bee, fee-bee."

I identify with this common bird. She lives in a world colored by finches, tanagers, and indigo buntings. Her simple song is surrounded by rippling warbles, the soft mourn of the dove, the eloquence of the purple martin, and the jeer of jays.

I rarely travel far on a journey of any type before I begin to compare myself with those around me. "Daughter," the Lord calls, "what is that to thee? Follow thou Me."

Yes, Lord, I want to follow You. Please forgive me for stilling my song when I look at those around me. (Sigh.) I am a daughter of Eve, acutely aware of my failures, prone to compare, intimidated at times by the abilities of others. Do I realize my potential as a daughter of God?

"Follow thou me." Jesus spoke these very words to simple fishermen. How He used those men! The scene, recorded in John 21, is familiar. Peter deserted the others and plunged into the water, eager to meet his Master again. After pulling in a net overloaded with fish, the other disciples joined Peter and Jesus on the shore.

(It seems they had returned to fishing in the absence of their Saviour.) Jesus addresses Peter, who had suggested they go fishing. "Lovest thou me?" Three times the question knifed Peter's soul as he wrestled with being a fisherman or a fisher of men. Turning away, Peter's eyes rested on "the disciple whom Jesus loved." His mind darted from the remarkable call he had just received from the Lord, to question what task might be given to his peer. "Lord, and what shall this man do?"

"What is that to thee? Follow thou Me," Jesus responded, commanding Peter's concerns to return to introspection.

I am comforted knowing that even the apostles wrestled with their natural tendencies in the pursuit of living in victory as sons of God. Yet it was their feet that carried the Gospel the first miles to reach the world. God entrusted the message to them, calling them to spread it at great risk to their lives. They rose to answer the call. Will I? Will you? God still entrusts humans with living for His glory and telling the Good News of the Gospel.

Entrusted me? Entrusted you? Yes, God's message is ours to share as well! Simplicity and modesty in dress, speech, and conduct can highlight our message. Finery and eloquence can be distractions. The message we have to share is too important to dilute or distort.

In Sincerity

D-A-U-G-H-T-E-R-Enter. Each time I type my password on my computer I am thankful for my daughter's blunder. Pushing a pencil felt fine for me. My family convinced me that a computer would speed up my writing. (They did not know how much that would confuse my brain!) "You will need a password," my teenage daughter informed me as she prepared my program.

"I'll choose 'daughter,' " I said, while my mind resisted the change.

"Are you sure you'll remember that?" She looked at me quizzically.

How could I forget? The ideas about being a daughter of Eve and a daughter of God had been chasing each other around in my mind for years. "I'll remember," I assured her.

"There is one problem," she said when she had finished, "somehow I typed your password in capital letters."

I smiled. Considering the trouble I was having organizing my seedlings of ideas, I expected I might forget to capitalize "daughter." But bearing in mind the natural struggle I face in balancing my life as a daughter of Eve and a daughter of God, I suspected the extra effort to capitalize the word daughter would be helpful.

I was right. My brain may be juggling thoughts, my heart may be questioning motives, I may be dealing with trying people or facing taxing circumstances, but when I sit down at my computer, typing "DAUGHTER" reminds me that I belong to God and He is sovereign. I am sincere about being His daughter. I can trust Him in whatever circumstances He has allowed.

Why focus on being a daughter? It reminds us we belong. It causes us to ask other important questions: If I belong to Him, then how should I live? What is my purpose as a daughter of God? Will what I am about to do bring glory to my Father? Am I sincere in living for Him?

With Purpose

What is our purpose in life? Print it boldly (capitalize it!) at the top of your list of priorities. WE WERE CREATED FOR GOD'S PLEASURE. "Thou art worthy, O Lord, to receive glory and honour and power: for thou hast created all things, and for thy pleasure they are and were created" (Revelation 4:11). Close your eyes and consider our awesome, mighty, holy Creator. Now think of yourself with your temperament, your personality traits, your heart, soul, mind, body—yes, all of you. You were created to bring honor and glory to God. What a remarkable opportunity!

"But I fail so often; how can God want me? How can He love me? How can I glorify Him?" Have you asked yourself any of the questions Ruby did, her eyes glistening with tears? Ruby's early journey as a daughter of Eve was marked by uncertainty and pain. Safety and security dwelled somewhere beyond the walls of her home. None of her family claimed a personal relationship with God, but from the time Ruby's little legs dangled from the bench at summer Bible school, she knew she wanted to be a part of this big family where the Father was God. The problem was that her experiences as a daughter of Eve kept getting in the way of understanding her position of victory as a daughter of God. Thoughts of self-condemnation and fear dragged her repeatedly to pits of discouragement.

"God loves you," Christians told Ruby as they tried to encourage her. *Why would He? Does He love me the way my family loved me? Is He waiting to hurt me? Does*

He care? Gradually her questions were answered. By burrowing into God's Word she found truth to replace her encumbered identity. She *purposed* to see herself as the cherished daughter of God that she was. Enfolded in His love, Ruby viewed her circumstances with new light. The things that troubled her invited her to grow in Christlikeness.

With Ruby, we all can realize a second purpose in life: becoming like Christ. God planned for us "to be conformed to the image of his Son" (Romans 8:29). The Christian's purpose in living is to identify with Christ, to "put on Christ" (see Romans 13:14 and Galatians 3:27). The "all things" that "work together for good" include the things that help conform us to the image of Christ (Romans 8:28).

A third purpose in life for the child of God is clearly outlined in Genesis 1:28. We were created to work. What daughter of Eve cannot find plenty of that?

We have a vital role in God's plan for mankind. Fulfilling these purposes in life, we do bring pleasure to God! The aroma of Christ wafts heavenward from daughters of God who serve Him with purpose.

And in Truth

In his article, "Destined to Soar," K. P. Yohannan states:

"There is no greater threat to Satan's kingdom than Christians who know and live their identity as sons and daughters of Almighty God. Satan is unable to stop or defeat such followers of Christ, unless he succeeds in stealing their knowledge of who they are in Him.

How does he do it? Through lies and deception. If the believer is not firmly grounded in the Word of God and does not reject the enemy's words, they will plunge him into a vicious cycle of deception. He will no longer see himself as a conqueror and ambassador for Christ, but he will assume the false identity the devil gave him and live in it."[1]

Fighting the enemy and his strongholds is impossible without assistance. Our greatest weapon is the Word of God; its truth attacks the towers of untruth that the devil builds in our minds. "For the weapons of our warfare are not carnal, but mighty through God to the pulling down of strong holds; casting down imaginations, and every high thing that exalteth itself against the knowledge of God, and bringing into captivity every thought to the obedience of Christ" (2 Corinthians 10:4, 5).

The tower of our God is higher and stronger than any stronghold of the devil. Even the Lord's name is a place of refuge. "The name of the LORD is a strong tower: the righteous runneth into it, and is safe" (Proverbs 18:10).

Harbored in God's mighty fortress of truth, we are shielded from the devil's darting weapons. Zinging past our ears, flaming arrows of untruth threaten to ignite condemnation or cause a false identity to smolder for years. From these smoky strongholds the devil strains to torment the child of God.

Run with me to the Strong Tower. Listen! I hear an echo from within the walls. Another daughter of Eve proclaims her true identity to the adversary: "I am a cherished daughter of God!"

Challenged, Cherished, Chastened Daughter

Challenged? Yes, we are continually being challenged as God's daughters. Cherished? The more we study His

19

Word, the more we see that His "loving-kindness [His cherishing] is better than life" (Psalm 63:3). And, yes, His cherishing is for me, for you. Chastened? We chafe at the thought, but even chastening reminds us of our marvelous daughterhood (Hebrews 12:5-7).

Amy Carmichael, whose suffering and life of sacrifice endeared her to Christ, wrote:

> I have a word of comfort for all who feel as if they will never be what their Lord wants them to be, and what they themselves want to be. It is, "He will thoroughly cleanse His threshing-floor." [Taken from Luke 3:17.] If only we spread out our whole being before the Lord, He will thoroughly deal with everything in us which is chaff in His eyes. The means which He uses are compared to the searching forces of wind and fire. We must not try to keep anything from the wind and the fire. If we are open like a threshing-floor, then nothing can hinder our Lord in His thoroughly cleansing work. One more word of comfort; the fan that makes the wind is in *His* hand—the hand that was wounded for our transgressions—and fire is only another name for burning love. Whatever the means of our perfecting may be, they come by way of His hand.[2]

Here in the Northeast, my phoebe friend is the harbinger of spring. Do I share a message of hope and new beginnings as well? Readily and with sincerity? Do I rest in and rise to God's purpose for my life? Do I focus on truth and live in the light of God's Word? Do I delight in being a daughter of God?

Daughter of Eve, come along on a journey in our quest to live as daughters of God. We have a magnificent message to share and an uncommon adornment to grace . . . simply, sincerely, truthfully. What purpose for our lives! "Fee-bee, fee-bee!"

Called to be daughters of purpose, we will examine, in the next chapters, specific ways we can be daughters for His glory.

Scriptures

Suggested Reading: Ephesians 3:14-21

"Sing forth the honour of his name:
make his praise glorious."
Psalm 66:2

"That they should seek the Lord,
if haply they might feel after him,
and find him, though he be not far
from every one of us:
for in him *we live, and move,* and *have our being* . . .
For we are also his *offspring.*"
Acts 17:27, 28 [emphasis mine]

"As many as I love, I rebuke and chasten:
be zealous therefore, and repent."
Revelation 3:19

"Now thanks be unto God,
which always causeth us to triumph in Christ,
and maketh manifest the savour of
his knowledge by us in every place.
For we are unto God a sweet savour of Christ."
2 Corinthians 2:14, 15

Prayer

Dear Father God,

How grateful I am to be your DAUGHTER! Help me to treasure that identity and live in its promise. I want to serve You in simplicity, in sincerity, and in truth. Help me always remember to run to Your tower of strength for protection from the enemy. I want to fulfill Your purposes for my life. I want to work, be conformed to the image of Christ, and bring honor and glory to You.

I want to be a fragrance of Christ to You, Dear Father.

Love from Your Daughter,

_____

WITH
STRENGTHS
AND WEAKNESSES

CHAPTER 3

I am Yours, Lord,

Femininely Yours

*H*ave you ever found yourself up to your forearms in a tub of sudsy water, scrubbing still another pair of sneakers or size ten, grass-stained jeans, and wondering why God created you a woman? As daughters of Eve, we are created to be "help meets," (see Genesis 2:18). Does such a helper for man only meet the growls of hungry stomachs, make order out of chaos, and be certain that children read with expression and wash behind their ears? We should not underestimate the value of these and other womanly jobs, but we may ask these questions: Are women created only to meet the needs of men and children? If I am unmarried or childless, if I am not a helpmeet to a husband, can I be fulfilled? What is my role as a woman?

In the Image of God

Formed from the dust of the ground, Adam named the animals and longed for a companion. As God Himself desired companionship, He recognized man's need of the same. So from the man God created woman. When Adam saw her, he said, "This is now bone of my bones, and flesh of my flesh: she shall be called Woman, because she was taken out of Man" (Genesis 2:23). *One* human had reflected the image of God; now *two* did, as male and female counterparts. Together men and women emulate the image of God. While it is true that woman was created to be man's helper, she was also created (in God's image) to worship, love, and glorify God in her uniquely feminine way.

Men reflect the image of God in strength, protection, provision, and leadership abilities. Women reflect God's creativity, compassion, sensitivity, and tender nurturing.

Whether or not you are married, your femininity provides balance in creation and is designed to glorify God.

Woman complements man. In areas where he is weak or unskillful, she is, by God's design, capable or competent; likewise, where she is weak, he is strong. When blended together, his needs evoke her strengths and her weaknesses draw out his abilities. (Who but God could have created this complementary existence so beautifully?)

Different by Design

In appearance, physical strength, and emotional composition, women are usually softer and more delicate than men. In an art class I attended with an artist friend of mine, we worked on drawing profiles. Below her darting pencil emerged a masculine profile like the one we were supposed to draw; mine looked strangely feminine.

"What am I doing wrong?" I asked her.

"Males are more angular. Your sketch is too soft. Make a man's nose and chin boxy. Use more straight lines and fewer curves."

I was amazed to see how these adjustments immediately changed the profile into a masculine one.

Men in general are rather like the male profile: comprised of direct lines and boxes. Their approach to life has been labeled "practical." Typically when a man sets a goal, he aims straight for the finish line. If interrupted or deterred, he somehow seems able to "box" the interruptions and his emotions and focus logically on the goal.

Generally speaking, women tend to flow along, focusing more on relationships. En route to a goal, a woman may curve off course and give in to the emotions of the moment. Women's approach to life has been labeled "emotional."

As straight and boxy lines convey masculinity, a man's practical, straightforward tendencies powerfully equip him to be the leader God created him to be. As curved, flowing lines denote femininity, a woman's sensitivities to emotion and relationships bestow on her the qualities best suited to be the nurturer God created her to be.

Allow me to illustrate.

Turtle Tellings

Today as I drove to the bus stop to pick up our schoolchildren, a very small turtle interrupted me. Poking his tiny head out of his shell, he took two slow steps onto the pavement. I contemplated rescuing the turtle for two reasons: First, my feminine sensitivity did not want him to get crushed. Secondly, as their nurturer, I knew my children would love to see the turtle or keep him for "show and tell."

I faced a problem: Was I brave enough to pick up the turtle? (Being afraid to touch creepy, crawly things is another common feminine characteristic!) I decided against the rescue—unaided by masculine courage—and hoped the turtle might survive until our return trip. My sons were happy to retrieve him!

Consider what a man's response might have been to the tiny turtle today. Most likely a man would have continued on his way without considering its welfare or how the children might use it. It may be best not to mention that some men might have decided to crush it.

Not every woman would have contemplated rescuing the turtle for some child to enjoy, nor would every man have passed it by without thoughts similar to mine. But generally speaking, stopping for a turtle while en route to a destination would have been a "curve" in the "box" of a man's day.

God had more than turtles in mind when He designed woman differently than man.

Different Roles

The ability to focus on goals and attain them is a quality well suited to men because God asks them to be leaders and providers. Men can more easily make decisions without being swayed by emotions. Their practical bent lends credibility to their leadership. Conversely, women's sensitivity, creativity, and other more relational qualities equip them to be excellent nurturers and helpmeets. Women make good mothers, teachers, nurses, and caregivers because we are inclined to relate to the feelings of others. Our sensitivity (not only for turtles) encourages us to listen to and empathize with those who are hurting, threatened, or sad. Our emotional bent lends heart to our nurturing.

Compare a list of masculine and feminine attributes. Men are empowered to lead and provide. Women are enabled to assist and nurture. In today's society some would argue with these statements, but the truth remains—men and women were created differently from the very beginning in order to fulfill their God-given roles. The daughter of God who accepts and submits to the differing roles of men and women rests in peace and grows in wisdom. The world frantically chases after "rights" and "equality" until men and women drown in a pool of confusion and disappointing consequences.

Feminine Fabric

Women may also be lovers of beauty, seekers of intimacy, feeling-oriented, and vulnerable. Quite often we have a deep spiritual sensitivity and a strong desire for an intimate relationship with God.

Whether kneeling in warm earth to plant flowers, snipping and stitching for long hours to make a quilt, or arranging the furniture in her home, a woman loves to make things beautiful.

At a former residence, I tended what I called my Jesus flower bed. It was graced with a dogwood tree, several rose-of-Sharon bushes, lilies of the valley, and an azalea that burst into bloom near Easter. Each of these plants reminded me of my Lord in some way, while the annuals I added offered their praises in steady bloom. Many women delight in partnering with God in gardening beautifully.

An 87-year-old friend of mine is sewing together 2,395 small patches of material to make a "Grandmother's Flower Garden" quilt. All of us know it would be much simpler to make a cover for warmth by sewing together two pieces of whole fabric with batting between them. But by expending great effort, my friend creates beauty for others to enjoy.

Methods of creating beauty are personal and distinctive. Regardless of the form you choose, you express your femininity by softening or beautifying your surroundings. Beauty should not be seen as the ultimate priority, though, and it needs to be balanced with practicality and moderation. (Guess whose attributes helps us with that?) Although it may need tempering, this desire for beauty is not wrong. It reflects our Creator, God.

Women also have a God-given desire for intimacy (defined as confidential friendship by the dictionary and understood by women as a deeper relationship than the practical aspects of day-to-day life). We may crave intimacy and go to great lengths to achieve it. Many women abandon personal freedoms or goals in order to become a wife and mother. We offer ourselves and our talents to benefit the lives of others. We change our names to that of our husband's, and submit to his leadership. We give sacrificially to our children not only in giving birth to them, but in raising them as well. In exchange, we hope to be loved and cared for, and we seek intimacy in these relationships. A married woman may have difficulty explaining this desire to her husband, but she is often keenly aware when this level of communication and relationship is absent. Likewise, single women may struggle with expressing their desire to married women, or they may wrestle with knowing what to do with their desire for intimacy.

To the amazement of most men, women are very aware of their feelings. When asked how they are feeling about something, women may launch into a detailed and heart-stirring account of their feelings, while men may honestly answer "I don't know." We may not always understand the reason for our feelings, but we women can usually verbalize them and frequently find ourselves piloted by them. Indeed, it takes great effort to rise above our feelings and focus on facts, something that often comes quite naturally to a man. Sensitive awareness of feelings contributes to a woman's relational skills as well as her nurturing abilities. Although this focus on feelings may at times be cumbersome to a man, it is a great asset to him in relating to his children and others. A woman's feelings, and her husband's recognition of them, also add immeasurably to the intimacy of marriage.

Women occupy a position of vulnerability in their place of submission to leadership. Exposing feelings and inner thoughts is risky business. It makes one *more* vulnerable. A woman may wonder: *will my views be acknowledged, appreciated, directed tenderly*? By candidly sharing her opinions and feelings, a woman gives of herself without knowing how she will be accepted or received. Being ignored, rejected, or criticized are all possibilities.

Sharing feelings and being vulnerable are risks many women agree to take in their search for intimacy. This transparency on the part of a married woman enables her husband to better understand her, and encourages growth in their relationship. For single women, being transparent and sharing in this way deepens and strengthens friendships with other women.

Often women are more spiritually sensitive than men. Have you pondered why God did not give this attribute predominantly to men since they are to be the spiritual leaders? I believe God had a special reason for giving this precious gift to womankind. He recognizes a woman's vulnerable position. Will the man take his rightful place in leadership? Will he lead her according to Scriptural principles with her best interest in mind? Will he care for her soul? The answer is "no" in some cases and "not always" in others. As women at times find it difficult to submit, so also men find it difficult to lead, and all men fail occasionally. As a result, some Christian women find themselves in the precarious position of having inadequate or poor spiritual leadership. At such times a woman can be extremely grateful for her deep spiritual sensitivity. It guides her to the never-failing, omniscient Leader, her Lord. There she can find the intimacy she desires, with a loving, heavenly Father, while being led and sustained by Him. In God she finds grace to submit to male leadership and courage to continue being vulnerable in her search for intimacy. "But my God shall supply all your need according to his riches in glory by Christ Jesus" (Philippians 4:19).

The human body is a marvel of complicated systems and coordinated action. Females are created by God with glands, organs, and hormones that facilitate childbearing and nourishment. A description of femininity is incomplete without mentioning that fluctuating levels of specific hormones contribute to a woman's overall feelings of well-being or distress. The word *hormone* comes from the Greek term *hormon,* which means "to set in motion."[1] In a woman's body, hormones set in motion many wonderful things, as well as some undesirable feelings. Our Creator is aware of our design and provides mercy and grace for our weaker moments.

Feminine attributes combine with the ways women are different from men, making women mysterious. Men may laugh about it, tell jokes about it, and be frustrated by it. But this feminine fabric also intrigues and fascinates them. While the differences may lead to misunderstanding and conflict, they also contribute to men's and women's attraction to each other and the balancing of their traits and tendencies. Even Agur, a writer of wise statements, considered that combination a mystery (see Proverbs 30:18, 19).

The Desire to Be
Understood and Appreciated

"Why doesn't he understand me?" is a common cry of daughters of Eve. We find it difficult to understand how the men in our lives do not readily understand and feel our emotions. While they box events or distractions and move on to deal with them practically and logically, we flow from one event to the next, carrying along the emotions from each one and focusing on how these things affect us and our relationships with others.

My day started smoothly enough. The family was off to work or school and my washing machine was swallowing multiple mounds of soiled laundry. Though rainy weather hampered my efforts, the jumbled piles gradually changed to neatly folded ones. Several phone calls produced babysitting and other necessary arrangements so that I might spend the evening and the next day with my husband. He had planned the business trip, but he wanted me to join him, and I was excited about spending the time with him. I even took some time to dream and plan between my detergent dumpings, phone calls, and household chores. *A business trip, yes, but it would be nice to do something special.*

During the afternoon things began to deteriorate — minor things, but irritations nonetheless. Interruptions. Unexpected problems needing to be resolved before I could leave. A missing ingredient for our evening meal. Then my husband arrived and casually announced a change in plans that would significantly shorten our time together.

I wish I could say I sweetly submitted to the change. But in typical feminine fashion, the flow of the afternoon's frustrations joined forces with the sudden and great disappointment. I reacted.

Sadly enough, the next day's shortened outing was marred by a breach in our relationship. My plans for something special became curves in the box of my husband's business day. His box of business plans stifled my curve toward relationship-building plans.

After seeking forgiveness from my Lord and my husband, and giving myself a firm talking to, I adjusted my expectations. Having decided to be happy with the box of a simple business trip with my husband, I enjoyed the remainder of the day. Released from the pressure to perform, my husband attended to his business and enjoyed my company. As I surrendered my will, I enjoyed being his true comrade and helper in business. I did paint pictures on the side of the box, though, by looking for bright or beautiful spots in the day, and confirmations of my husband's love. After all, I am a woman.

A woman longs to be heard, understood, comforted, and assured of security and acceptance. She wants to feel and know she is loved. If a man fails to recognize or deal with these issues and desires, a woman may become frustrated and angry. Feeling insecure and unsure of herself, she may lash out or try to control. This in turn threatens a man's sense of leadership or accomplishment. In response, he may either lash out or withdraw into a shell. The woman feels less understood. The man becomes more confused. Beware: dangerous downward spiral ahead!

Contention

"Contentious" is defined as a quarrelsome spirit. Patterns of angry and controlling responses make a contentious woman, and that which she desires moves further from her grasp. The Bible compares such a woman to a constant dripping (annoying) and says it is better to live on the rooftop without her! (See Proverbs 27:15 and 25:24.)

Glenda experienced emotional wounds and rejection in her childhood. When she married, she hoped to fill the void that stalked her life. But before long she faced the familiar sting of pain and rejection. Glenda responded by developing controlling patterns—pushing people away as a means of protection, or pulling them toward her to meet her perceived needs. She was headed down the road of becoming a contentious woman when God arrested her attention with a simple verse, "Every wise woman buildeth her house: but the foolish plucketh it down with her hands" (Proverbs 14:1). Convicted that she was tearing down her husband and young children, Glenda repented of her sin and sought God's face, asking Him to meet her strong desires and unfulfilled longings. Cradled in God's love, she turned to travel the road to recovery.

None of us set out to be contentious women. We do not want to drive our husbands or families to the housetop. A single woman may find herself being contentious about not having a husband. Then people around her may also find the housetop comforting.

How should a daughter of God respond to the

frustrations of feeling unheard, ignored, or rejected? So much of Eve remains inside us. Where do we go with the sensitive feelings and emotions God has given us? Should we deny them, stuff them deep within, and resign ourselves to this lot in life? How do we fight the urge to contentiously control?

Heeding Hannah's Example

Hannah of the Bible gives us a wonderful example of how to maintain our God-given sensitivity and bring our desires to the Lord. As a daughter of Eve, Hannah agonized over being childless. To add to her dismay, her husband's other wife taunted her. (If you have despaired at infertility, you know the ache of unfulfilled longings and the sting of unkind remarks.)

Hannah talked to her husband about her desires. His words to her, "Am not I better to thee than ten sons?" (1 Samuel 1:8), must have hurt as well. Apparently sons were important to him, for he had married another wife to obtain them. Imagine Hannah's distress when her heart cry was unheard by her husband. She could have built a wall and closed herself to the pain, squelching her sensitivity. She could have rejected her husband's love. (He did love her and even gave her a double portion of the meat from his yearly sacrifices in Shiloh.) Hannah could easily have become contentious. Instead, she packed up her anguish and bitterness of soul and went along to the temple. There she poured out her sensitive, feminine soul, with its gnawing desires, before her Lord (1 Samuel 1:10).

At home her cry was unheard; now it was criticized. The priest Eli accused her of being drunk. Hannah explained, "I am a woman of a sorrowful spirit: I have drunk neither wine nor strong drink, but have poured out my soul before the Lord." While men misunder-stood, God heard Hannah's cries and saw her tears. His finger traced the jagged edges of her broken heart. Pleased with her vow, God decided to give Hannah the desire of her heart. Before she left the temple, Eli blessed her with a promise: "Go in peace: and the God of Israel grant thee thy petition that thou hast asked of him" (1 Samuel 1:17). After asking for grace, Hannah returned home with a changed countenance and a vibrant hope. God's comfort settled around her and His blessings began to bloom.

Delighting to Surrender

Not only does God give daughters of Eve sensitive, emotional souls, He also places in us deep longings and intense desires that encourage us to come to Him in utter brokenness, dependence, and surrender.

As we pour out our longings and desires before God, we must also be willing to surrender to His will. When Hannah arose from her prayer, she had a promise. Could she believe it? Could she surrender and fulfill her vow? As we follow the account in 1 Samuel, we see Hannah rejoice in submission. She fulfilled her vow by bringing her answer to prayer back to the temple. This time she sang a song of praise to God. What would enable a woman to sing praises when she faced separa-tion from her only child? Only the grace of God. While carrying and weaning young Samuel, Hannah experi-enced a powerful work of God. He transformed her from a weeping, desperate woman to a committed, praising saint.

Hannah's circumstances could have precipitated contentiousness. Instead, she became calm and com-mitted. Is it any wonder God blessed this daughter of

His with five more children? He delighted in her. He gave her the desire of her heart; for she had come brokenly to Him, trusted Him to provide for her, and learned to delight in Him.

Psalm 37:4 proclaims, "Delight thyself also in the LORD; and he shall give thee the desires of thine heart." Is this a promise you and I can claim? Will God answer our prayers precisely and then give us five times more than we asked for, as He did for Hannah? Yes, it is a promise we can claim. No, God will not always answer our petitions in the way He did for Hannah. But as we delight in Him, God blesses us and fulfills the desires of our hearts in the ways He sees best. Or He may change the desires of our hearts to that which agrees with His will. Delighting in God includes the willingness to surrender to His will.

Delight and surrender? They seem like opposites to many women. But God's grace enables us to do just that: delight in Him and surrender to His will. Gladness follows.

Truly, as daughters of God, we are comforted so that we can sing with Hannah: "My heart rejoiceth in the LORD . . . . Neither is there any rock like our God" (1 Samuel 2:1, 2).

Feminine for God

Womankind was created by God with special attributes and for special purposes. In His great mercy and loving-kindness, God plants within us deep longings and desires, such as the longing for male spiritual leadership and the desire to mother children. These desires are designed to drive a woman to her knees in utter dependence on God. He knows she is safest there.

God wants us to serve Him in our uniquely feminine

way and thus bring glory to His name. As He did for Hannah, God delights in blessing obedient, committed daughters far beyond our imagination.

Woman was the first to sin in taking and eating that which was forbidden in the Garden of Eden. Thousands of years later woman was also first to see the risen Lord in another garden. Christ's first recorded words after Resurrection were: "Woman, why weepest thou? whom seekest thou?" (John 20:15). God cares about the tears of women.

God loves you as a daughter. He understands and delights in your femininity. He longs to have you surrender and delight in Him.

Scriptures

"And the Lord God said,
It is not good that the man should be alone;
I will make him an help meet for him."
Genesis 2:18

"Bring my sons from far,
and my daughters from the ends of the earth;
Even every one that is called by my name:
for I have created him [or her] for my glory."
Isaiah 43:6, 7

"The sacrifices of God are a broken spirit:
a broken and a contrite heart,
O God, thou wilt not despise."
Psalm 51:17

"I waited patiently for the Lord;
and he inclined unto me, and heard my cry."
Psalm 40:1

"I delight to do thy will, O my God:
yea, thy law is within my heart."
Psalm 40:8

Prayer

Dear God,
You created me as a woman. I have attributes that reflect
You. I was created with the potential to be a sensitive nur-
turer of children and a "help meet" to a man.
Thank You that, whether I am married or single, my fem-
ininity provides balance to Your masculine creation. Thank
You that You value me as a woman, Your daughter. By Your
grace, I want to achieve my greatest potential – to glorify
Your Name by serving You in my uniquely feminine way.
You created me with godly longings and desires. Some-
times these are unfulfilled. When I find myself unheard, dis-
appointed, or brokenhearted, help me to be like Hannah. May
I come to You in brokenness. I want to delight in You; then
you can give me the desires of my heart. I know You will not
always meet my desires in the way or at the time I expect
them to be met. I give You permission to change my desires
if You so desire. Give me grace to surrender to Your will so
that my life will be a testimony as Hannah's was.
Keep me from contentiousness.
I want to be known as a woman of God.

Femininely Yours,

_____

CHAPTER 4

Lord, sometimes
we are . . .

Painfully Yours

Cuddled in my arms, her sobbing subsided slowly. When my daughter rolled a ball toward her, Wendy smiled. Squelching the last sob with a deep sigh, she slid off my lap and toddled over to reach for the ball. Though a brief scene in this adopted child's life, I hoped it foreshadowed a greater healing.

"Throw the ball to me, Wendy; you can do it!" my daughter encouraged. Wendy chuckled as she filled her short arms with the ball and lunged forward, trying to throw it. To her delight it dropped at her feet and rolled several inches. The little girl tottered for a moment until the force of her efforts sent her sprawling to the floor beside the ball. Before her distressed look became a wail, my daughter picked her up and praised her for her accomplishment; then, encircling the toddler in her arms, she helped Wendy throw the ball again.

As Wendy's babysitters, we could ease her pain of separation for a few hours; but in life Wendy faces a bigger struggle. Already she has experienced surgery and frequent hospitalizations. Unprotected from the drugs and alcohol that coursed through her biological mother's veins and into her own tiny, developing body,

Wendy bears the marks of someone else's sin. She pays a price for her birth parent's poor decisions.

What will Wendy's future hold? Will bitterness take root and strangle spiritual growth? Will her spiritual growth be stifled by becoming comfortable with being a victim? Or will she take her tears, totter off to God, and reach for His healing? Someday, maybe she will strain to thrust a ball of hope toward someone else who is hurting. Yes, she will fall at times, as we all do, but God will be close by with open arms and ready encouragement. I pray Wendy will reach for victory.

We women are touched by the suffering of this young daughter of Eve. We understand why she clings to her adoptive parents or wrestles with fear. Do we also recognize that these early childhood experiences will have a profound effect on her life, possibly into adulthood? Will we insist that she dry her tears, stuff her pain, and be a "proper Christian"? Or will we roll her a beautiful ball of hope? When she and other daughters of God stumble under the weight they carry, will we declare that the past has no bearing on their present struggles? For fear of falling prey to deceptions of modern psychology, will we pull away from those who suffer? Or will we encircle them in love and offer hope?

Before we sweep anyone's distress — Wendy's or our own — under a rug of denial, we should ask a question we may wish to avoid: "Why?" (If you cringe to ask why, remember that Jesus in agony, cried from the cross, "My God, why hast thou forsaken Me?" Someone suggested that asking *why* is not wrong, but demanding an answer is.) If you are suffering, the daughter of Eve in you is already asking "why." Maybe it is time to explore the "why" hand in hand with the God who claims you as His daughter. Why do we suffer? What purpose, what potential, lies hidden in our miseries?

Putting a Handle on Adversity

Consider this collection of quotations:[1]

- "Adversity is God's university." —Paul Evans
- "If God is in charge and loves us, then whatever is given is subject to His control and is meant ultimately for our joy." —Elisabeth Elliot
- "The presence of Christ puts pain in perspective." —David L. Thompson
- "Only the willingness to suffer can conquer suffering." —David J. Bosch
- "Teach me, dear God, the glory of my cross; teach me the value of my 'thorn.' Show me that I have climbed to Thee by the path of pain. Show me that my tears have made my rainbow." —George Matheson

Learning, perspective, conquering, a path to God— do we recognize the training school of suffering? Do we prize the glory, joy, and rainbows hidden in hurting?

Pain, adversity, affliction—whatever we may call it— we all experience it to some degree. "Yet man is born unto trouble, as the sparks fly upward," says Job 5:7.

How do we handle pain and adversity? Ignore it? Pray that we will not be bothered by it? Wallow in it? React to it in ways that harm the next generation? Or do we see a cross (or a rainbow) and hear a call to Christlikeness rising from our suffering? Have you visited the university of adversity? The curriculum is individualized, so likely yours will differ from mine.

Of Dolls and Losses

One day, years ago, I recaptured painful pieces of my childhood.

43

My two young daughters were sitting side by side on the sofa with a large Christmas catalog spread open on their laps. Hearing their exclamations, I smiled, guessing they were browsing the doll section. I joined them to reminisce and learn of their interests.

Action dolls were posed by bikes, skates, or other accessories. Fashion dolls sported the latest hairstyles and clothing. But my girls were attracted to the lifelike dolls that waited to be cuddled.

Suddenly I remembered myself as a pigtailed girl with a similar catalog. My desires were the same; I wished for a new doll to cuddle and care for. When Christmas came there was a large gift waiting at Grandmother's house. It was from my father, who lived there. Timidly, I unwrapped it as he watched. I could not recall ever receiving a gift from him.

Remembering the cute, cuddly dolls from the catalog, my heart danced with anticipation. Had Daddy seen me admiring them? When the gift wrap was gone, there was a doll; but it was so very different from the one I had hoped for. It was stiff-limbed, ready for action, and dressed like a boy. My heart stumbled and fell to rest somewhere in the pit of my stomach. Bravely I smiled and thanked Daddy for the doll. I showed him how she tumbled and pushed her own little car with her stiff, rotating arms. "Tumbling Tomboy" the doll was called, and away tumbled my dreams.

Most of the time that doll stayed in its box. Years later, I found the doll in the attic, and I understood my aversion to it. My hopes and dreams went far deeper than a new doll. I had hoped for a secure, united home to replace my broken one. I had dreamed of a close relationship with my father, who had angrily left our home when I was five. Though I could not have explained it on that long-ago Christmas day, the doll was so much like what my father had given me of himself. He seemed cold and aloof; his lap unwelcoming. Like the doll, whose stiff, rigid arms prevented cuddling, something seemed to hold me away from his heart. To add to my disappointment, the doll's boyish clothes reminded me of the schism in our home. My mother was raising me in a Mennonite church and teaching conservative values. My father bitterly opposed the church and denied the assurance of salvation. Conflict was inevitable.

Both of my parents had, in fact, experienced adversity and the loss of their own fathers at a young age. I came to understand later that my father's distancing me and our family was one way he coped with unresolved issues in his own life. He had built walls to protect himself, but inside he seethed with anger. As a young child I did not understand my father's struggles, but I was keenly aware of the walls. Proverbs 17:6 says " The glory of children are their fathers." That glory held empty spots for me. Within my heart the longings grew, and the pain my dad had known in losing a father became my pain as well.

I longed to be cherished and protected by my father and to experience his spiritual leadership in our home, but my longings went unfulfilled. Unanswered questions distressed my soul, and without realizing it, I began to feel angry as well. Already my misery seemed certain to affect another generation, for surely my anger, if unresolved, would someday distance me from my children. What was I to do with the pain that produced the anger?

Somewhere between the time the Tumbling Tomboy doll was put into the attic and the day I found it again, God, in great mercy, began to lead me on a journey toward security and acceptance. Gently He taught me about the value of pain and adversity. Sitting beside my young daughters and remembering the doll, I paged through more than a catalog. God's comfort washed over me as I reviewed mile markers on my transforming journey of healing. As a young mother, I was filled with hope. I could trust my heavenly Father to guide me safely on. I thanked God that my parents had been reunited shortly before I married, and I determined to continue praying for my father's salvation. Sometimes it seemed improbable that he would ever lay his burden of bitterness at the foot of the cross. But, enabled by God's grace, I could break the chain of sinful responses and their damaging consequences; I could do more than just cope—I could find victory and peace!

Daughters of Need

As a young person I assumed that "normal" Christian families did not experience the hurts and unfulfilled longings I knew. I was wrong. People may suffer painful experiences in either believing or unbelieving families. Created by God as emotional humans, we are quite easily wounded and angered by our experiences. Wounded people tend to wound others.

Melissa was raised in a believing family and became a member of a conservative church where her father was ordained a church leader. She often fell prey to her father's explosive anger. Not wanting to expose his errors, the family absorbed and covered his sin. Melissa knew she should honor her parents, and outwardly she did, but inwardly she grew increasingly angry and confused at his inconsistencies. To protect herself she learned to build walls and distanced herself from her family. Now, as a married woman, Melissa has discovered that she still tends to build walls to protect herself from close, intimate relationships with her husband and children. Years of hardening herself against the pain of mistreatment left her heart numbly callous. While hardening provided a protection of sorts, it prevented her from experiencing the joy of healing and victory.

Do elements of your journey threaten to steal your joy and thwart your growth as a child of God?

Coping Only?

As daughters of Eve, we cope with our sufferings in a variety of ways: We may blame others for our problems. We may give way to emotion and harm others with destructive anger. We may manipulate circumstances or pressure people, so that we control outcomes. Or we may claim we're victims to avoid responsibility for our own actions. We may withdraw into protective shells and distance ourselves from pain and people. Or we may harden our heart so that painful things will not hurt so badly.

These methods of coping have three things in common: First, all are aimed at self-preservation rather than submission to the will of God. Second, none provide the profound healing and comfort God offers. Third, patterns of coping tend to develop gradually, taking firm root in our behavior and choking out desire for a better way.

Coping seems to get us through tight spots — or around them — but it shortchanges a true solution to our problem.

Consider two Biblical daughters of God and their responses to affliction.

Naomi's Grief

When Naomi returned to Bethlehem with only her Moabitish daughter-in-law, Ruth, the people asked, "Is this Naomi?"

She replied, "Call me not Naomi, call me Mara: for the Almighty hath dealt very bitterly with me. I went out full, and the LORD hath brought me home again empty: why then call ye me Naomi, seeing the LORD hath testified against me, and the Almighty hath afflicted me?" (Ruth 1:20, 21).

The name *Naomi* means "my delight," while *Mara* means "bitter." Naomi is sometimes charged with turning her back on God in full-blown bitterness. Before we harshly criticize her, we need to consider how we might have responded in her circumstances.

Her husband had taken her, possibly against her will, to a heathen country in order to avoid the plight of famine in their own country. There she knew the heartache of watching her two sons marry heathen women. Isolated from family and God-fearing friends, she faced, not only the death of her husband, but also the untimely deaths of her only children. Can you imagine a greater burden of grief than that borne by Naomi? Her remarks upon arriving in Bethlehem were cries of anguish from a deeply grieving heart. She did not denounce God. Although she accuses Him of sending her home empty, she still addresses Him as "Almighty."

Naomi was grieving and faced depression and hopeless despair. She could easily have prayed with the psalmist: "The troubles of my heart are enlarged: O bring thou me out of my distresses. Look upon mine affliction and my pain; and forgive all my sins" (Psalm 25:17, 18).

Had God forsaken Naomi? Was her situation truly

hopeless? Chapter 2 of the Book of Ruth shows us a dramatic change in Naomi.

Naomi's Comfort

God promised Israel in Isaiah 66:13, "As one whom his mother comforteth, so will I comfort you." Tenderly, God comforted Naomi. Coming home "empty" was not completely empty, for Ruth came with her. Ruth was willing to leave her country, her relatives, and her heathen gods so that she might cling to Naomi and her God. What a blessing Naomi found in this God-seeking daughter-in-law! Ruth's willingness to humble herself and work for their living by gleaning barley was a first glimmer of hope. When Ruth returned home at the end of a long day with a promising harvest and leftovers from a meal she had been given, Naomi's hope burst into praise. "Blessed be he that did take knowledge of thee"(Ruth 2:19). Added to Ruth's earnings for the day was the gift of Boaz's kindness. She had earned his deepest respect and admiration. Naomi's hope soared, for she remembered the practice of redeeming. (Redeeming occurred when a near relative bought the land of his relative's widow and, if she was childless, he commonly chose to marry her in order to raise up seed to inherit the land.) "Blessed be he of the LORD, who hath not left off his kindness to the living and to the dead," Naomi responded joyfully. She realized God had *not* forsaken her (2:20).

Naomi's of Today

Can you identify with Naomi? Or are you abundantly blessed and find yourself perplexed at how to relate to the afflicted? Too often we are critical, as we tend to be of Naomi. We offer encouragement and suggestions to put the past behind and move on. We may say with resignation, "Life is like that," and piously quote, "All things work together for good" (as if we can somehow sever it from the other rich truths of Romans 8), dispensing it as a quick cure. Such responses offer little hope to the Naomi's we meet.

With or without the support and understanding of others, those who are hurting can diligently search for and relish the personal promises God has scattered through His Word — handfuls of grain just waiting to be gleaned.

Gleaning Golden Grain

What messages lie waiting to be learned in the affliction or suffering we face? Like Ruth, we can humble ourselves and glean — not barley, but truths from God's Word. We will find a loving Lord and Master, like Boaz, who longs to exercise His redeeming power and extend His healing hand. May I share some golden grain I found while gleaning?

Our suffering or adversity:

1. Is part of God's plan. "For he hath not despised nor abhorred the affliction of the afflicted; neither hath he hid his face from him; but when he cried unto him, he heard" (Psalm 22:24). God does not despise affliction. Our first glimmer of hope is realizing that God has a purpose for our suffering.

Does that mean all our trouble comes from God? Is He dutifully dispensing it as a pharmacist would some distasteful medicine? Proverbs 17:3 says "The fining pot is for silver, and the furnace for gold: but the LORD trieth the hearts." But wait; read on.

2. May be from the Father, the devil, or our choices. God is not the creator and dispenser of all our pain. Some comes straight from the devil and the effect he has had on the lives of others. "Wherefore, as by one man sin entered into the world, and death by sin; and so death passed upon all men" (Romans 5:12).

Some suffering is the result of our own sinful choices, and becomes a consequence God uses for chastening His dear child. "And ye have forgotten the exhortation which speaketh unto you as unto children, My son, despise not thou the chastening of the Lord, nor faint when thou art rebuked of him: for whom the Lord loveth he chasteneth, and scourgeth every son whom he receiveth. If ye endure chastening, God dealeth with you as with sons; for what son is he whom the father chasteneth not?" (Hebrews 12:5-7).

"Behold, happy is the man whom God correcteth: therefore despise not thou the chastening of the Almighty: for he maketh sore, and bindeth up: he woundeth, and his hands make whole" (Job 5:17, 18).

3. Is for our profit. Being joyful about chastisement is difficult, but God displays His great love and mercy as He wounds us so that we may grow in grace and be spared from the clutches of evil. He does it "for our profit, that we might be partakers of his holiness." Then, "afterward it yieldeth the peaceable fruit of righteousness unto them which are exercised thereby" (Hebrews 12:10, 11).

When experiencing adversity, ask God to reveal, through His Spirit, whether He is chastising you. His forgiveness will follow your honest confession, and your growth will be fruitful in righteousness!

4. Is for yielding fruit. Godly character is another fruit of adversity. Some pain is allowed by God in order to produce godly character in our lives. "It is good for me that I have been afflicted; that I might learn thy statutes" (Psalm 119:71). Adversity is a powerful character refiner.

Affliction has the potential to make us more Christlike. "That I may know him, and the power of his resurrection, and the fellowship of his sufferings, being made conformable unto his death" (Philippians 3:10). Enduring suffering and dying to self (including the urge to protect ourselves from pain) identifies us with Christ. See 1 Peter 4:12, 13.

5. Is for usefulness in the Potter's hand. At the potter's house, Jeremiah watched the potter create a vessel out of clay by spinning it on the potter's wheel. "And the vessel that he made of clay was marred [blemished] in the hand of the potter: so he made it again another vessel, as seemed good to the potter to make it" (Jeremiah 18:4). Strong hands destroyed the first vessel, squeezing and kneading the soft clay. After placing it again in the center of the wheel, the hands carefully formed a new vessel. The Lord spoke to Jeremiah as he watched and said, "Cannot I do with you as this potter? . . . Behold as the clay is in the potter's hand, so are ye in mine hand, O house of Israel" (v. 6). God desired to remake the nation of Israel. He longed for her to be yielded to His skillful hands.

"But now, O LORD, thou art our father; we are the clay, and thou our potter; and we all are the work of thy hand" (Isaiah 64:8). Each of us, as daughters of God, sits on His wheel. As the Master Potter, He is sovereign and can remake our marred and blemished vessels. Our part is to be yielded, soft clay in the Master's hand.

We can be absolutely certain that regardless of how we became marred or blemished, God wants to remake us into useful vessels for His honor and glory.

6. Is more precious than gold. Yes, God has purpose for that which tries our faith. "That the trial of your faith, being much more precious than of gold that perisheth, though it be tried with fire, might be found unto *praise* and *honour* and *glory* at the appearing of Jesus Christ" (1 Peter 1:7, italics added). Not only does a potter remake a vessel, he also bakes it in a hot oven (two or more times) before it becomes a finished product. Finishing or refining is a painful process, but the finished product is more precious than gold! Go ahead and shine for the glory of God.

A Journey

In my personal walk through affliction, I traveled through mile markers of understanding and yieldedness.

First, I faced my hurt honestly. When hidden, it had erupted at unexpected times or in uncomfortable ways, so it felt threatening to examine it openly. In this part of the journey God allowed people to come beside me who were insightful and willing to walk with me through self-examination. The insights they provided were more valuable than my own warped perspective.

"Is any among you afflicted? let him pray" (James 5:13). Earnestly I prayed. I asked God to remake my marred vessel and heal the wounds. I asked for His divine intervention in breaking patterns of behavior that were crippling to growth.

I mourned. "Blessed are they that mourn: for they shall be comforted" (Matthew 5:4). An important step in my healing process was learning to mourn, rather than wallowing in self-pity. I mourned the loss of my father's presence in our home. I grieved for the close relationship we could have had, and the family we could have been. God spoke comfort to me through His Word, through His Spirit, and through other Christians.

I discovered that grieving was helpful at different stages of my life. I grieved for the little girl I had been and the losses I had experienced at that time. I grieved as a teenager when I began those first steps of self-examination. I grieved as a young mother who wished for the maturity and confidence a united home would have given. More recently, I grieved again as I sat by my father's grave, trusting in my heavenly Father's love and merciful grace. (If you are wondering, more of my father's story is included in later chapters. I faced his grave with joy as well as sorrow.)

Along my journey, I learned that persistent, self-absorbing grief is not conducive to true healing and growth. Sometimes circumstances are ongoing and mourning is extended. But prolonged pain or affliction is tempered by God's mercy and grace when we humble ourselves to receive it.

God helped me see the futility of wallowing in self-pity and the hopelessness of using my circumstances to excuse sinful behavior. Why be content as a victim when God called me to be a victor?

I also learned the rich treasure of God's comfort and the truth that "weeping may endure for a night, but joy cometh in the morning" (Psalm 30:5).

All along the journey, forgiveness was a very vital part of healing. If I did not forgive those who had wounded me, I was easy prey for the lion of bitterness that lurked, waiting to devour my soul. Forgiveness is difficult for daughters of Eve, but we can honestly tell God that we do not feel ready to forgive—and then ask Him to make us willing. We choose to forgive, but it is God's grace that helps us make that choice.

Again and again I forgave. I recognized God's goodness in allowing me the opportunity to grieve and forgive on an ongoing basis. I could see that it had refined my character and softened my hard heart. Brokenness brings blessings. God values a broken and contrite heart (see Psalm 51:17).

Grieving enabled me to accept my losses. The more I studied what the Bible has to say about affliction, the more I realized God had allowed my experiences for a reason. His perfect will did not include a broken home, but He allowed it. When I accepted my past with its imperfections, I knew a peace that passed the world's understanding.

Accompanying that peace was the joy and thrill of seeing how God was able to use my experiences to minister to others. Second Corinthians 1:3-5 became life verses for me: "Blessed be God, even the Father of our Lord Jesus Christ, the Father of mercies, and the God of all comfort; who comforteth us in all our tribulation, that we may be able to comfort them which are in any trouble, by the comfort wherewith we ourselves are comforted of God. For as the sufferings of Christ abound in us, so our consolation also aboundeth by Christ." Pain had deepened my compassion, and I really was able to comfort others with the comfort God had given me. I was able to move beyond *acceptance* of my past to *praise* for the way God had led. I thanked Him for adversity. I praised Him for His healing. I humbly marveled at the opportunities He gave me to extend His comfort to others.

A surprising element of my journey has been the

value of looking back. Probing into one's past is frowned upon by some Christians, insisted upon by others, and exercised cautiously by most. I found that looking back helped me understand myself and my responses. Even more encouraging was tracing God's hand at work throughout my life. I still marvel when I review His omniscient direction and His outpouring of grace.

One precious truth I gleaned by looking back is how God graciously turned my heart toward Himself. In my real lack of male spiritual leadership, my heart turned to seek God. Decades after I walked through those turbulent adolescent years, I realized that God had helped me choose several godly men from area churches to serve as father images. It was not until I sat at the funeral of one of those men and reflected on my past, that I saw how God had thus blessed me in a way that helped me develop a healthy understanding of who He was. My soul would have missed that blessing had I not taken the courage to look back.

Looking back is not without risk. The devil may use this exercise to trap us in a preoccupation with our past or a selfish wallowing in the pain. He endeavors to keep us self-pitying victims. Carefully God pulled me from bogs of such bondage.

Looking back also provides a hint of where God is leading me. I recognize my susceptibility and strong reaction to rejection by looking honestly at my past. I know that God will faithfully bring things into my life that will teach me to deal with rejection and the strong feelings it evokes. As I prepare this manuscript, I am very aware that writers frequently receive rejection slips. It's interesting that God asked me to write. He is asking me to trust Him even in the face of rejection. These thoughts are not inserted here as a special note to editors but as a reminder to me that God has every right to faithfully edit and direct my life. He calls me to hurdle my fears.

Jesus cautions about plowing while looking back (Luke 9:62). You may have heard someone use this verse to caution against looking back at one's past. I was surprised to look at the context and discover that this verse is grouped with other cautions regarding the difficulty of discipleship. Looking back with a reluctance to move ahead snags the person who is called to serve in the kingdom of God. But at the end of a furrow, hand in hand with God, you too may be surprised how good it is for your soul to look back and reflect on God's faithfulness.

Psalm 107:8, 15, 21, and 31 repeat the glorious message: "Oh that men would praise the LORD for his goodness, and for his wonderful works to the children of men!"

God allows affliction in our lives to weed out sin, produce humble brokenness, and bring praise to His name. Along with goodness, pain and affliction are part of God's wonderful works to the daughters of God.

Make a Well

Some of you readily identified with this chapter. My prayer is that you will allow God to lead you on a journey to acceptance, healing, praise, and usefulness. Afflictions vary, as does the journey, but the Map is detailed and personal. Travel on by its guidance. Rest long in its precious promises. Experience the rich treasures of God's goodness. When you pass through a valley of Baca (weeping), make it a well (Psalm 84:5, 6). Draw from your tears to refresh yourself and others.

Openhanded Living

Have some of you had difficulty wading through

this chapter? Perhaps affliction is not something to which you relate. "Should I pray for affliction?" you might ask.

Experience life with open hands and live in God's will. If blessings are taken away, grieve, but continue to trust Him. Should affliction pierce your path, accept it with open hands. Then squeeze it with all your might to receive each drop of goodness God has hidden there. From the pen of twice-widowed Elisabeth Elliot:

> The important thing is to receive this moment's experience with both hands. Don't waste it . . . . The effect of my troubles depends not on the nature of the troubles themselves but on how I receive them. I can receive them with both hands in faith and acceptance, or I can rebel and reject. What they produce if I rebel and reject will be something very different from a mature character, something nobody is going to like.[2]

As daughters of Eve we are tempted to grasp our blessings with white-knuckled fists. Daughters of God learn to relax in His love, extending fingers slowly to raise tender palms to Him. "Thy will be done."

Tempted, Tried, and Triumphant!

You will be tempted, as I am while I write this. A situation has arisen that awakens past feelings of fear and rejection. My faith trembles; but it stands. Again His grace is being extended to me. As I review what is written I can say "Amen" to His will for my life, for I see His hands at work — this Gentle Potter who desires to make me more like His Son.

"But we see Jesus . . . crowned with glory and honour; that he by the grace of God should taste death for every man. For it became him, for whom are all things, and by whom are all things, in bringing many [daughters] unto glory, to make the captain of their salvation perfect through sufferings" (Hebrews 2:9, 10). As the Captain of our salvation, Christ submitted to intense suffering. If God so allows, will you submit to suffering so that He can use you to minister to others?

If God allows, little Wendy will grow up. In adolescence she may recoil or react in frightening ways to the suffering she's experienced. Other daughters of Eve will also suffer. Rejection. Damaging criticism. Abuse. Their journeys as daughters of God may be torturous and slow. Will you roll a beautiful ball of hope toward them? Will you encourage them on their journey of healing? Will you take steps on your own journey?

Scriptures

"For we have not an high priest which cannot be
touched with the feeling of our infirmities;
but was in all points tempted like as we are,
yet without sin. Let us therefore come boldly unto
the throne of grace, that we may obtain mercy,
and find grace to help in time of need."
Hebrews 4:15, 16

"Blessed is the man whose strength is in thee;
in whose heart are the ways of them.
Who passing through the valley of Baca
make it a well."
Psalm 84:5, 6

"Heal me, O LORD, and I shall be healed;
save me, and I shall be saved: for thou art my praise."
Jeremiah 17:14

"For I reckon that the sufferings of this present
time are not worthy to be compared with the glory
which shall be revealed in us."
Romans 8:18

Prayer

Dear Sovereign Potter,

*I am yours — a lump of clay that You wish to form into a
vessel for Your honor and glory. As I spin on Your potter's
wheel I wish to stay soft and pliable. Peel away any hardness
of heart. Remake my vessel as You see fit. Help me to accept
both blessing and affliction openhandedly so that I might be
refined and redeemed.*

*Your Word says, "Many are the afflictions of the right-
eous: but the LORD delivereth him out of them all" (Psalm
34:19). I do not ask that You would spare me from affliction
or a painful past. Give value to them as only You can do.*

*When I am tempted, help me to claim Psalm 32:7, "Thou
art my hiding place; thou shalt preserve me from trouble;
thou shalt compass me about with songs of deliverance."*

*Help me to rest in Psalm 32:8, "I will instruct thee and
teach thee in the way which thou shalt go: I will guide thee
with mine eye."*

*When I pass through a valley of Baca help me make it a
well, drawing refreshment for myself and others. Thereby
may Your name be glorified.*

*And, Lord, I want to praise You for Your goodness and
Your wonderful works to the daughters of God!*

Praising, even when Painfully Yours,

CHAPTER 5

Lord, I want to be—

Meekly and Quietly Yours

*T*hrough my kitchen window, I saw the large blue coffee can sitting precariously in our backyard. I made a mental note to remind our children to return it and its curious contents to the neighbor child who had brought it to our lawn the day before. "Look what I found," he had shouted excitedly as he peeled back the lid so that we might peek inside.

There among leaves and twigs rested a very large caterpillar. My children had responded with similar enthusiasm to the green artistically-decorated worm that was as large as their dad's finger. We readily agreed that the excited boy should take it to "show and tell." But as first graders are prone to do, he had absent-mindedly deserted the can and skipped home after playing ball.

I winced, remembering that days earlier I had quickly closed our front door when this child bounded up the steps to ask permission to play with our boys. My older children had chided me for my less-than-hospitable response, and my younger children had dejectedly continued their chores. "We've had enough interruptions for today," I had stated emphatically, trying to justify myself. My conscience tingled and I confessed to my family that, indeed, I should have responded in a more kind and mannerly way. Where was my meek and quiet spirit? To make amends I decided to accompany my children when they returned the canned caterpillar.

To our surprise, the caterpillar was nowhere to be seen. A brown web-like "nest" clung to the side of the coffee can. The distinctive caterpillar had built a cocoon or chrysalis. The children's delight and curiosity grew.

Knowing that the ugly caterpillar would soon change into a beautiful moth or butterfly gave me a sense of hope. My responses, not only to interruptions but also to the stresses of life, can change as well. An ugly attitude can metamorphose into a lovely meek and quiet spirit. How?

Growing Character

Unlike the caterpillar that makes one cocoon and experiences a lasting dramatic change, daughters of God develop a meek and quiet spirit over a process of time. It is not inborn.

For years I wrestled to understand how I could stuff my bubbly, outgoing, passionate personality into a meek-and-quiet-spirit box. John Coblentz's definitions of meekness and quietness, and his explanation of the difference between "personality" and "spirit" help me understand just what it is that God desires of me:

"**Meekness** is being humbly submissive, especially in response to God or to the circumstances or people He has allowed in my life.

"**Quietness** is being calm in my spirit—peaceful at

the core—even in the midst of the storm." John and his wife, Barbara, further described a quiet spirit as "an absolute surrender to God, knowing that God is able to turn my turbulence into peace."[1]

When wild waves come crashing in rapid succession over my craft—can I really be "humbly submissive" and "calm in spirit"? Those are tall orders for daughters of Eve, regardless of our personality types.

While some women are born with quiet *personalities*, or are by nature meek in temperament, all daughters of God need to work hard at developing meek and quiet *spirits*. For some of us meekness and quietness seems especially elusive because we have personalities that are outgoing and vivacious. We may be talkative, excitable, opinionated communicators. Is meekness and quietness beyond our reach? And what about women who are naturally quiet—bashful, shy, or reserved? Or women who are calm, mild, and compliant in disposition? Is it correct to assume that they are also meek and quiet in spirit? The answers are "no." Meekness and quietness are possible for all daughters of God, whether they demonstrate it in bashful or in bubbly ways. And no one receives a meek and quiet spirit automatically, based on her personality traits.

First Peter identifies the *spirit* of meekness and quietness; that is, the *character*, rather than the *personality* of women. "Whose adorning let it not be that outward adorning . . . but let it be the hidden man of the heart, in that which is not corruptible, even the ornament of a meek and quiet spirit, which is in the sight of God of great price" (1 Peter 3:3, 4). We are *born* with the personality traits God gave us. We *grow* character, deep in our spirit.

Quiet, reserved Annette remained quietly reserved while caring for her aging, failing parents. But her spirit felt anything but meek and quiet. "Where is God when I need Him?" she asked dejectedly. She wrestled with the circumstances that were forced upon her. God had provided an opportunity for her to develop a meek and quiet spirit.

In contrast, vocal, outgoing Audrey shared her turbulent feelings with her friends and wept often as she watched her husband succumb to a terminal illness. But inside she felt an unexplainable peace. "I just know God cares and that He will see us through this ordeal," she confided. Her testimony gave evidence of her growth in the ornament of a meek and quiet spirit.

Annette and Audrey are women with two different personalities, evidencing different spirits. One displayed a meek and quiet personality; the other, a meek and quiet spirit. God calls all daughters of His, regardless of their personalities, to grow in the spirit of meekness and quietness.

Review again the definitions of meekness and quietness as quoted earlier. As daughters of Eve, we long to be peaceful at the core. But how can we be peaceful in insecure situations? While it is natural for us to desire peace and security, it is contrary to our nature to develop meek and quiet spirits.

The Search for Peace: Naturally

Daughters of Eve tend to tread two well-paved paths to what we perceive as peace and security. One path is a walk of control. Inwardly or subconsciously, we tell ourselves: "I want to have security, therefore, I will do _____ and I will not allow _____ to happen to me or my family." (Think about how you might fill in the blanks.)

In search of peace and security, women may become controlling. We may boss, nag, scheme, and manipulate rather than humbly submit to God and the circumstances He has allowed in our lives. As daughters of Eve, we tend to try to control our environment and the people whose decisions affect us. This behavior, although it may appear to get results, is not ornamental, nor does it testify of our faith and trust in God. Continued attempts to control eventually lead a woman farther from the deepest desires of her heart.

"I just want him to love me and provide a good home for our children," complains one troubled woman. She attempts to control the amount of time her husband is away from their home and criticizes his failures as a father. As a result, her husband spends less time at home and becomes emotionally distant from his wife and children. What this woman most desires moves farther from her grasp.

The second well-paved path to supposed security is one of complacent endurance. This is not to be confused with the glad surrender, sweet submission, and joyful acceptance that a meek and quiet spirit brings. In contrast, it is a resigned, that's-just-the-way-life-is attitude. Although it may be perceived as quiet, this behavior is also not ornamental. God's plan becomes something to be avoided or quietly endured.

"I can't do anything about it," explains another troubled woman, "so I just keep quiet." She simply endures the disappointment of wayward sons. What was meant to drive her in faith to God through intercessory prayer is simply accepted and endured. And in this way we may miss God's best for us.

We do well to evaluate our motives and actions and then humbly (meekly) ask ourselves: Is there a better way to reach for the peace and security I desire?

The Supernatural Provision of Peace

There is an ornamental way. God prizes it. As daughters of God, we can delight in adding the ornament of a meek and quiet spirit to our varied personalities.

In the world, an ornament's value is determined not only by its beauty but also by the difficulty with which it is procured and perfected. Considering that a woman can labor with God her entire life to develop a meek and quiet spirit, and perfect it as a response to the stresses of life, it is little wonder that God calls it an ornament of great price!

How do we obtain a meek and quiet spirit? Demand it? Certainly not. The Bible says "Ye have not, because ye ask not." And further: "Ye ask, and receive not, because ye ask amiss, that ye may consume it upon your lusts" (James 4:2, 3).

The first step in obtaining a meek and quiet spirit is to ask God for it. We ask, not only because we want to receive the benefits, but also because it will bring glory to God. His amazing grace will strengthen us in this area of natural weakness.

"The meek shall eat and be satisfied: they shall praise the LORD that seek him." (Psalm 22:26). Meekness comes by seeking God and being satisfied with His will.

"The meek will he guide in judgment: and the meek will he teach his way" (Psalm 25:9). We obtain meekness by having a teachable spirit.

When we (1) ask for this ornament, (2) seek God's face, (3) learn to be satisfied with His will, and (4) humble ourselves to being taught of His ways, then we adorn ourselves with the ornament of a meek and quiet spirit.

John Coblentz identifies five prerequisites for meekness: "Meekness comes by:

- knowing that God is in control of my life,
- knowing that God is able to change my situation,
- turning the reins over to the one who is in charge,
- knowing that God can keep my situation exactly as it is, and He can still be sufficient to meet my every need,
- knowing that GOD IS THAT BIG."[2]

Reread the above five statements. Now think of a situation or circumstance in your life that threatens to destroy your peace and security. Talk to God about it. Make statements out of the above phrases. *"Dear God, I know that You are in control of my life, even when I feel so out of control. I know You are able to change my situation if You so desire. Give me strength and help me to turn the reins of this situation over to You and to _____."* (Name the person who should be in charge, if that is the case; for example, your husband or your minister.)

"I know You can keep my situation exactly as it is and that You will give me grace sufficient to meet my every need. God, You alone are that big!"

Sometimes I need to repeat these statements several times or for several days. As soon as I can (and maybe even before I feel able to), I thank God for the difficult circumstances. I acknowledge that He may not have caused them, but He allowed them. I remind myself that God wants to build my character and draw me close to Himself. In the quietness of my spirit, I surrender myself and my circumstances to God. God's grace really is sufficient to turn our turbulence into peace!

MQS Guides and Charts

You may wish to make a "meek and quiet spirit guide" to keep in your Bible. On an index card write the five "Meekness comes by" statements and the definitions of meekness and quietness. You may write a prayer, leaving blanks for the details and specifics. Then the next time you are faced with something to which you feel like reacting, reach for your guide and seek God's face. Pray the prayer you have written, filling in the blanks with the current events and details. Humble yourself to being taught by this situation. Smile. You are well on your way to developing a meek and quiet spirit.

At one time, my daughters and I kept what we called our "MQS Chart." On it were our names and when we had encountered situations that called for a meek and quiet spirit. My maturing daughters had printed 1 Peter 3:3, 4 carefully at the top of the chart. Our MQS chart helped us strive together to adorn ourselves in the way God desired. When my grown daughters reminisce, they mention the MQS chart. It made its mark. Perhaps it is time to post another chart of this nature in our home, for a meek and quiet spirit should be a lifelong pursuit of godly women. I could use a visual reminder again.

As you strive to develop a meek and quiet spirit, you will be rewarded. "But without faith it is impossible to please him: for he that cometh to God must believe that he is, and that he is a rewarder of them that diligently seek him" (Hebrews 11:6).

Use Adversity for Advantage

Meek and quiet spirits may lie dormant when everything is going our way. Adversity brings opportunity to grow. Romans 5:1-5 speaks to this:

"Therefore being justified by faith, we have peace with God through our Lord Jesus Christ: by whom also we have access by faith into this grace wherein we stand, and rejoice in hope of the glory of God. And not only so, but we glory in tribulations also: knowing that tribulation worketh patience; and patience, experience; and experience, hope: And hope maketh not ashamed; because the love of God is shed abroad in our hearts by the Holy Ghost which is given unto us."

The storm of adversity causes the turbulence. A quiet spirit, drawn from faith in God, brings peace.

At ninety years of age, Mary is frail and aching physically. Slowly, with cane in hand, she walks to the second pew of her church. Arthritis, heart disease, and age have weakened her body. But her spirit is vibrant and strong. When testimony time comes, her weaknesses are evidenced only by speaking slowly and remaining seated while she talks. The congregation is reverently quiet, listening for her words of wisdom. She always begins with praise to her loving Lord. Faith beams strong and true as she testifies of His grace; her face radiates peace. Obviously, the joy of the Lord is her strength.

For many years this saint sought the face of God and adorned herself with a meek and quiet spirit. Her life was not one of ease or plenty. The man she married became deceived and grew obstinate. He accused her of causing him to distrust the Lord. While he refused to work, she provided meagerly for their two young children by sewing for others. Eventually her husband left her, totally neglecting her and the children's needs. "My Lord was my helper," Mary says of those difficult years. "He still is," she continues with conviction; "He has never failed me." By God's grace Mary has surrendered to God's will and used her adverse circumstances to develop a meek and quiet spirit. Added to her outgoing personality and love for her Lord and others, Mary's spirit bubbles over with gratefulness. Even at ninety her adornment is beautiful!

Surrendering Sarah

Sarai or Sarah, ancient daughter of God, and wife of Abram or Abraham, also surrendered. Her God-ordained protector and provider deserted her when he feared for his own life. It could not have been easy for Sarai to submit to her husband's request to identify herself as his sister when they drew near to Egypt. According to Genesis 20:12 Sarai was Abram's half sister, so he was not asking her to lie completely; but the reason for his request must have wounded Sarai's heart, making her aware of her vulnerability: "Behold now, I know that thou art a fair woman to look upon: therefore it shall come to pass, when the Egyptians shall see thee, that they shall say, This is his wife: and they will kill me, but they will save thee alive. Say, I pray thee, thou art my sister: that it may be well with me for thy sake; and my soul shall live because of thee" (Genesis 12:11-13).

So Abram hid his true identity, and Sarai was noticed by the princes and commended before Pharaoh. Did Sarai call Abram a coward? Did she attempt to control him so that she would be safe? It appears from the account that she surrendered to his leadership even though she must have questioned it, especially when she was taken into Pharaoh's house. The Lord was protecting this daughter of Eve, even if her husband was not. The Bible says, "The LORD plagued Pharaoh and his house with great plagues because of Sarai Abram's wife" (12:17). Before Pharaoh was able to make her his wife, he discovered that Sarai was more to Abram than a sister; she was his wife. I wonder, did Sarai—alone, forsaken, and held in a foreign palace—disclose the information to Pharaoh? How must Abram have blushed when Pharaoh demanded: "Why didst thou not tell me that she was thy wife? . . . Now therefore behold thy wife, take her, and go thy way" (12:18, 19).

Sarai's surrender to Abram's poor decision allowed God to work on Abram's selfishness. In the following chapters of Genesis, we note that Abram very unselfishly offered his nephew Lot the first choice of land, rescued Lot, and demonstrated unselfishness to the king of Sodom.

Sarah Seeks Control

Sarai did not always surrender easily and display a meek and quiet spirit. She was also tempted to control people and circumstances around her. When God's promise of a son for Abram was not forthcoming, Sarai decided to intervene. Her attempts to control spoke of her lack of faith: "I am old and God is not quite that big" (quote mine). Her plans to forcefully fill the promise resulted in rejection, anger, rebellion, and thousands of years of animosity between two people groups.

When three angels met with Abraham outside his tent, Sarah laughed to herself when she heard their promise that she would bear Abraham a son. Later, in fear, she denied it, saying, "I laughed not." Her laughter and doubts were stilled. Over the next months and years of her life, Sarah must have swelled in faith and glad surrender. Was it easy for her to respond in submission and adorn herself with a meek and quiet spirit? Probably not any easier than carrying and birthing a

71

child at the age of ninety.

In the words of the three mysterious visitors, "Is any thing too hard for the Lord?" (Genesis 18:14). When Isaac was born, Sarah said, "God hath made me to laugh, so that all that hear will laugh with me" (Genesis 21:6). This laughter was joyful, faith-filled laughter. (My God *is* that big!) It is echoed through the centuries by daughters of God who have learned the value of submission, surrender, and the adornment of a meek and quiet spirit.

Even as Sarah

First Peter 3 begins with challenges for wives to be in subjection and for women to adorn themselves with meekness and quietness; it continues with these verses: "For after this manner in the old time the holy women also, who trusted in God, adorned themselves, being in subjection unto their own husbands . . . even as Sarah obeyed Abraham, calling him lord: whose daughters ye are, as long as ye do well, and are not afraid with any amazement" (also translated: not "panicked" with any "sudden calamity").[3]

Who of us cannot relate to Sarah of old? Sometimes we seek to control; sometimes we doubt the bigness of our God. Always we have the opportunity to gladly surrender to God's plan and grow in meekness and quietness.

Etched into my memory is one year when I had ample opportunity to grow in this way. My father had suffered a stroke, and nine months later, he died.

After years of prayers, my parents had been reunited, ending fifteen years of separation. Though my father was still plagued by bitterness, he had taken steps toward God and had mellowed with age. For twenty more years we longed for him to have a complete surrender and commitment to Christ. Then, in the midst of rapidly declining health, he came to the end of himself and became a new man in Christ! Oh, the joy of watching him lay down that burden of bitterness!

For several glorious months we watched him become strong, even while his body wasted physically. Then the stroke. Again his life was altered. At first he was childlike: uninhibited, sincere, and lacking in knowledge. Although it was painful to see him lose so much, we rejoiced in the opportunity to learn to know him in a new way. This man, whom I'd longed to hear pray, now prayed ardently and aloud — simple, sincere prayers, full of unanswered questions, but blossoming with faith.

Then slowly, as more strokes robbed his intellect, he succumbed to cruel anger and intense selfishness. For five months we endured long, painful hours, day and night, of caring for a demanding, disparaging man. The storm of grief and pain was intense as he hurled verbal daggers at my mother and our family.

Self-abasing conclusions I'd made in my childhood were now verbalized with sharp accusations. My spirit wanted to cry out, *No, no, this cannot be happening.* But it was, and circumstances were beyond my control. I ran frequently to the arms of God, where my prayers became much as my father's had been: sincere, full of unanswered questions and growing faith. God comforted me and gave extra measures of grace for those difficult days, helping me to humbly submit to the circumstances He had allowed in my life. The storm was real and raging, but inside there was a welcome and unnatural calm. I asked for more grace and surrendered the situation to God, knowing He alone could fulfill Romans 8:28. I also came boldly to the throne of grace with several specific requests:

"God, have mercy on his soul; You know his mind has failed. Lord, take him home when You see fit, and give us the grace and strength to patiently endure until that time. And please, Heavenly Father, let our father's dying words to us be loving ones."

God faithfully answered my prayers, even the last request, which somehow seemed so important to me. My dad's last recognizable words to me were: "Goodbye and I love you." He spoke more after that; but the words, though spoken earnestly and with feeling, were unrecognizable, so much so that I wondered if they were words of my grandfather's native tongue, so foreign they were to me. In those moments I felt strongly the presence of God. Quite possibly God confounded Dad's speech for those minutes before I left his room. He died less than twelve hours later, after speaking clear and caring words to all other family members.

Although I would not have chosen the circumstances, God had allowed them, so I was confident He had a reason. Gradually, I came to see that the pain I suffered at the end of Dad's life led me to a deeper and more complete forgiveness and healing. His stormy death could have shipwrecked my soul if I had not cried out for meekness and quietness.

God's rest was available for our family's test. We learned important lessons about faith and forgiveness; God's mercy and grace sufficed for the trial. During the storm, the next generation witnessed the calm peace of their parents. For all of that "working together for good" God is to be praised!

Trapped for Transformation

Remember that caterpillar in the blue coffee can? Do you also feel trapped in your situation or circumstances? Do as the caterpillar did—build a cocoon. Get alone with God and wrap yourself in His Word. Meditate on the faithfulness of God. Review other times in your life when He used adverse circumstances to build character in your life and increase your faith. Thank and praise Him for your deliverance from those circumstances, or for the grace He gave you to submit to the circumstances and use them for His glory. Remember, God wants to do the same for you in the present circumstances.

Trusting God to deliver or enable you in your present storm requires faith. Faith is not merely believing hard enough that your anticipated, desired answer comes to fulfillment. Faith is more than that. When my faith is tested I have frequently reviewed this definition of faith as given by John Coblentz in a sermon that helped calm my troubled heart.

"Faith is trusting and believing that:
1) God IS.
2) God is GOOD.
3) God is ABLE.
4) God is able to use the people, circumstances, and situations in my life to:
   - draw me closer to Himself (James 4:6-10),
   - encourage growth and blessing in my life (James 1:2-4, 12),
   - minister to the needs of others (2 Corinthians 1:3-5),
   - and bring honor and glory to His name (1 Peter 1:7)."[4]

Respond with this level of all-encompassing faith to the circumstances that trouble you. Know that God is able to do marvelous things. Wrapped tightly in the cocoon of devotion to God, praise Him for your past deliverance or enabling. Thank Him for solid faith for today. You will soon burst forth gloriously — beautifully-winged and resting quietly in God's love. Do not rush away to fix, control, or matter-of-factly accept your circumstances. Rather do as the butterfly does when she has emerged from her chrysalis. Rest in the sun and exercise your wings, allowing them to dry and strengthening them for flight. Exercise praise and adoration. Exercise faith. Exercise meekness and quietness. By God's grace you will fly — above or around the storm that troubles you, or possibly through it — remembering that "underneath are the everlasting arms."

Now that is a safe way to fly! Fly on, daughter of Eve, in the meek and quiet ways ordained for daughters of God. "The eternal God is thy refuge, and underneath are the everlasting arms" (Deuteronomy 33:27).

Scriptures

"The LORD redeemeth the soul of his servants:
and none of them that trust in him shall be desolate."
Psalm 34:22

"The meek shall eat and be satisfied:
they shall praise the LORD that seek him."
Psalm 22:26

"Then they cry unto the LORD in their trouble,
and he bringeth them out of their distresses.
He maketh the storm a calm,
so that the waves thereof are still.
Then are they glad because they be quiet;
so he bringeth them unto their desired haven.
Oh that men would praise the LORD for his goodness,
and for his wonderful works to the children of men!"
Psalm 107:28-31

Prayer

Dear Master of the Seas,

As storms rise unexpectedly on the sea, stormy relation-ships or situations sometimes mark my life as well. In my hu-manness, I find myself reacting to the people, circumstances, or situations that trouble me. Inside I churn like the agitated waves. My peace and security are jarred.

Instead you ask me to grow in Christlikeness and to re-spond with a meek and quiet spirit. This is so unnatural for me as a woman, but You identify this character quality as an adornment of great price. Heavenly Father, I humbly ask that You would adorn me in this way. Help me not to attempt to control or complacently endure but to use the adversities in my life to develop meekness and quietness. Enable me to respond in faith, knowing that You are able to change my cir-cumstances or use them for Your honor and glory and my growth of character. May I laugh with Sarah of old, delight-ing in knowing that You really are that big!

Meekly and Quietly Yours,

_____

CHAPTER 6

Lord, help me to be—

Contentedly Yours

*A*s meekness and quietness are misunderstood, contentment is misrepresented. In today's world it is portrayed more as a curse than a virtue—something to be overcome rather than embraced. The world beckons: "You deserve more. You owe it to yourself. You will be happier if . . . " Advertisement urges us to improve, get more, and keep up with, or get ahead of, our neighbors. When this attitude of discontent marches boldly into our churches as well, the Christian's testimony of God's peace is marred.

In God's Word, contentment always has been and always will be a virtue to be cultivated. "But godliness with contentment is great gain," Paul tells Timothy in 1 Timothy 6:6. Where contentment is addressed in Scripture, meekness is often mentioned as well. Daughters of God do well to recognize the "great gain" of this virtue and—along with meekness and quietness— adorn ourselves with the positive character quality of contentment. Truly meek and contented women are rare jewels today. Happy is the man who finds one. More importantly, the God they serve is glorified.

What Is Contentment?

The dictionary defines "contented" as being submissive to circumstances, accepting, resigned, satisfied. Contentment is being satisfied with things as they are. Then am I content if I refrain from painting my peeling porch, purchasing a desired item, or cleaning my cluttered attic? Not necessarily. I may be unmotivated, slothful, or busy with more important projects. Financial difficulty or time restraints may limit my ability to proceed with the tasks at hand. Contentment is *accepting* my peeling porch or cluttered attic while being satisfied to wait until circumstances allow me to remedy these problems. Contentment is being satisfied to wait until I can afford that desired item or being willing to do without it. Contentment is not simply avoiding tasks or resigning myself to limitations or circumstances. Rather, it is *deciding* to be satisfied, when my natural inclination is to demand change or to get what I desire.

A Biblical definition of contentment may be gleaned from 1 Timothy 6:6-11. Contentment here includes:

- Recognizing things as temporary. We cannot take them with us when we die (v. 7).

- Knowing that food and clothing are enough (v. 8).

- Realizing that the desire to be rich brings temptations and snares. It may destroy us and result in eternal damnation (v. 9).

- Remembering that "the love of money is the root of all evil." This love may well pierce us with sorrow and destroy our faith (v. 10).

As children of God we are to run from the snares of discontentment (v. 11): "But thou, O man of God, flee these things; and follow after righteousness, godliness, faith, love, patience, meekness."

Discontent: Scenes and Sources

Daughters of Eve are tempted to be discontented with their relationships, their personal appearance, and the appearance of their homes. True, some displeasure may prompt us to read relationship-building materials and set goals to improve our relationships. A measure of dissatisfaction may motivate us to exercise, lose weight, take calcium, or eat healthy foods. It may motivate us to shine windows, organize drawers, paint ceilings, or otherwise improve our homes. But an ongoing attitude of discontent is destructive, encumbering the soul. It places undue stress on a family or individual. ("He that troubleth his own house shall inherit the wind" Proverbs 11:29.)

The devil loves to try to tempt and trip contented Christians. He may use a variety of means to achieve this goal; four common ones are convenience, clutter, comparison, and the pursuit of pleasure.

Convenience Congests Contentment

Our world has changed. Things have become temptingly convenient. Your mother or grandmother may have taken a rare trip to town to stock up on necessary staples. This was a carefully planned event. If she was missing an ingredient for her evening meal, she borrowed from a neighbor or did without. If an essential article of clothing tore, it was patched rather than replaced. If shoes were outgrown, hand-me-downs were worn, or toes endured pinching until the funds and time were available for that next trip to town. In her words, she learned to "make do." Today, increased income, more vehicles, and a wider selection of local merchants, have made it convenient to quickly go to a store to complete, replace, and revitalize any number of things. We find it difficult to be content and make do as Grandmother did.

Technology has confounded our world with convenience. Modern appliances have automated chores that required significant effort to perform fifty or one hundred years ago. Free time is swallowed up by more functions, meetings, and social events. Or it is consumed by efforts to acquire, use, clean, or service the latest gadgets and timesaving appliances. We can also travel great distances, enlarging our circle of acquaintances and responsibilities. Simple pleasures may be forgotten as we catch the next plane or answer a rush of E-mail. Before we realize it, our lives become congested with that which is now so convenient.

Clutter Clouds Contentment

"I don't have time to read a story now," I informed my young daughter. Her gleaming eyes clouded.

"It's okay; I will help you work," she responded cheerfully after a few moments of dejection.

At the end of the day, I said prayers with her as I tucked her into bed. As she closed her eyes I thought of the anticipation they had mirrored earlier that day. I remembered then that I had gone from one task to the next all day long and had not read my daughter a story. I reviewed the work I had done. Was it all necessary? Could some of it have waited for another day? Did my home have to be super clean and tidy in order to host tomorrow's guests?

When our days become so cluttered with busyness that we cannot take time to enjoy simple things, our view of peaceful contentment is clouded. Our domestic cares sometimes obscure the importance of simply serving others contentedly.

The clutter of *things* can also draw us away from Christlike contentment. We remember the story of the prodigal son and how he walked away from God and the security of home. I was surprised to learn that the word "prodigal" actually means extravagant or addicted to wasteful expenditure. Might we also be labeled prodigal in our search for newer, better, and *more*?

"And [Jesus] said unto them, Take heed, and beware of covetousness: for a man's life consisteth not in the abundance of the things which he possesseth" (Luke 12:15).

Comparison Competes With Contentment

Probably more than anything else, comparison competes with contentment. Recently I was reminded of this in a personal way.

I closed the door of our large old home — comfortable and full of character, obviously lived in by a family. I visited an acquaintance in her new, immaculate home with a carefully manicured lawn. When I returned, my home looked far less appealing — messy, and in need of repairs. Quickly I picked up some books and slid them into their rightful places on the bookshelf. I began giving orders to the children to put their things away. "If that mother can keep her home neat and orderly, I should be able to as well," I verbalized my thoughts and emphatically stressed the importance of my family's cooperation. In a few short hours I had developed a raging case of "the comparison flu."

My feverish attempts to immediately organize my house and coerce my family into tidiness were interrupted by my daughter's quiet words of wisdom.

"Mother, her house may be neat, orderly, and appealing, but she is not writing a book." Her comment wiped my brow like a cool, wet washcloth; the furrows relaxed. I stopped to observe. It was true. Part of the disorder was mine. Some of the projects and tasks were unfinished because I had been writing.

"You are right," I told my daughter, giving her a quick hug. After apologizing, I changed my critical commands to pleasant requests. Together we worked at restoring order but with a new purpose in mind. We finished tasks and cleared the clutter for order's sake. I stopped demanding it for comparison's sake. God gently reminded me that the woman whose home was very neat and orderly could frequently and unashamedly host visitors without a lot of frenzied preparation. She could encourage others by hosting them in her tidy guest room; I could encourage others by writing in my disarranged back room.

A considerable part of contentment is accepting our individual differences and refraining from comparing with others. We are tempted to compare not only houses, but also faces, families, finances, abilities, backgrounds, wardrobes, blessings, blunders, and on and on. Second Corinthians 10:12 admonishes us well: "For we dare not make ourselves of the number, or compare ourselves with some that commend themselves: but they measuring themselves by themselves, and comparing themselves among themselves, are not wise."

The Pursuit of Pleasure

Pleasure seeking and entertainment are priorities in today's culture. While considered important industries, entertainment and recreation do not make people industrious. A steady diet of worldly entertainment does more than curb one's worthy accomplishments—it leads to discontent, as the enjoyment of simple pleasures is hindered by the compelling urge to do more thrilling things. Any woman who cares for children accustomed to hours of television or video viewing knows the difficulty of keeping them content. The creativity, resourcefulness, and imagination of these children are diminished in their demand to be entertained.

Pleasure seeking continues into youth and adulthood. Recently a young man said of our church's young people, "They seem so happy. But what a boring life – they can't do anything." The people of whom he spoke are not bored; they are content to do a great many things that do not seem exciting, thrilling, or tempting enough to a young man who has feasted on entertainment junk food.

While all pleasure seeking is not evil, it needs to be carefully kept in check. Like the seed that fell on ground that sprouted thorns, we may be "choked with cares and riches and pleasures of this life, and bring no fruit to perfection" (Luke 8:14). Paul warns Timothy of coming apostasy in 2 Timothy 3. His list of things to expect in such perilous times includes "lovers of pleasures more than lovers of God."

Do we have the courage to ask ourselves, "How much do I love and seek after pleasure?"

Discontent at Home

Discontentment in the home is readily passed on to the next generation. Many mothers have wondered why their sons or daughters demand the newest entertainment, insist on following the latest styles, and demonstrate annoyance with a life of simplicity as taught by the Bible and the church. Too often this attitude of discontent and annoyance has been learned, for it is modeled by adults. Do we insist on the latest and the finest for our homes? Are we attracted to magazines that tempt us to pour our energies into that which is applauded by the world? Is our modesty evidenced in dress only? Are we constantly seeking ways to increase our income or improve our social standing? If so, we may expect to see discontent, indulgence, and self-gratification repeated or magnified in the next generation.

Attitudes of discontent in the home, and in the church, confuse onlookers, especially if we try to convince them with words that we as Christians are called to be God's special, redeemed-people, separate from the world. Which kingdom—the kingdom of God, or the kingdom of this world—has preeminence in our lives? "Let your *moderation* be known unto all men. The Lord is at hand" (Philippians 4:5, emphasis added).

Cultivating Contentment

Daughters of God can cultivate contentment in many ways. First, we need to focus on Christ. He lived a life of self-denial and sacrifice so that men might be saved. Is it Christlike to live a life of self-gratification and self-indulgence while distancing ourselves from the needs of the souls around us?

Second, it is essential to remember that our residence in this world is *temporary*. Christ said His kingdom is not of this world (John 18:36). Furthermore, He prayed for those who did believe, and those who would believe, on Him: "I have given them thy word; and the world hath hated them, because they are not of the world, even as I am not of the world. I pray not that thou shouldest take them out of the world, but that thou shouldest keep them from the evil. They are not of the world, even as I am not of the world." (Taken from Christ's prayer recorded in John 17.) As daughters of God we are citizens of the kingdom of God. Our focus is on the life to come.

Third, it is vital that we seek affirmation and commendation from God and His Word, rather than demanding it from other people. Sometimes when we feel especially vulnerable we lean toward others, grasping for praise to bolster our wobbling self-worth. But even other Christians will fail us at times, and the world is not to be trusted in deciphering kingdom business or determining the worth of a child of God. In contrast, God and His Word never fail.

Blessed is the daughter of God who seeks for and finds direction and affirmation from her Father God in His Word! Relying on approval from other people is risky, and we have already examined the dangers of comparing ourselves among ourselves. The Scriptural alternatives are also found in 2 Corinthians 10. "Casting down imaginations, and every high thing that exalteth itself against the knowledge of God, and bringing into captivity every thought to the obedience of Christ" (verse 5). Seeking the approval of peers and comparing ourselves with others frequently includes imaginations and distortions. It is far better to compare ourselves to God and seek His approval. "For not he that commendeth himself is approved, but whom the Lord commendeth" (verse 18).

A fourth way to cultivate contentment is to train yourself and your children to enjoy simple activities. Suggestions abound. You may enjoy anything from reading books aloud (to your family or a blind senior) to hiking nature trails. Count the various birdsongs you hear in a day, or take time to pop jewelweed seedpods in the fall. In the bustle of busy days, and amid the din of the computer age, daughters of God should remember to treasure simple pleasures.

A secret of being content is to experience what I call "glarrow"—part gladness and part sorrow. Paul says in Philippians 4:11 "For I have learned, in whatsoever state I am, therewith to be content." He assures the Philippians that he knows how to be abased, and how to abound; how to be hungry, and how to be full; how "both to abound and to suffer need." Paul knew the gladness of ready provision. He also knew the sorrow of emptiness and need. Through Christ's strength (Philippians 4:13) and Paul's acceptance of both gladness and sorrow, a clear testimony of contentment was given.

In areas where you are tempted with discontentment, thank God for the "glarrow." Praise Him for the things about your appearance, your home, and your relationships or abilities, that make you glad. Remember to thank Him also for allowing the things that sadden you. God uses the mixture of gladness and sorrow, provision and lack, abounding and suffering need, to cultivate contentment in our lives.

Contentment, along with the joyful acceptance of the "glarrow" in our relationships—especially our marriages, gives a mighty message of Christ's love for the church. Do not miss the opportunity to paint a picture of Christ's sacrificial love through the tiny, everyday brush strokes of contented love in your home. (Read about specific brush strokes in Chapter 9.)

Daughters of God can cultivate contentment by carefully monitoring their reading material. Many magazines and books are designed to make us discontented. They entice us through advertising, pictures, or articles to change or improve our appearance, clothes, abilities, homes, and gardens. While change and improvement are not always wrong, a spirit of discontent is. Unchecked, our time can be consumed in perfecting our personal world while neglecting spiritual growth, personal evangelism, and teaching children godly character.

Finally, learn to balance work and pleasure. Not only were we created to bring glory to God, we were also created to work. In Genesis 2:15, God puts Adam in the garden to "dress it and to keep it." Only after Adam and Eve sinned did work become toilsome labor, "by the sweat of your brow." Contentment does not come by continually searching for entertainment and recreation but by balancing work and play.

Home – Haven of Contentment

We can use any of a number of ways to transform our homes into havens of contentment. One way is to set the table for mealtime and eat together. This time of sharing food and thoughts provides a continuing sense of satisfaction and contentment. When days scurry by with appointments and scheduling conflicts that prevent sharing one or more meals together, family members feel disjointed and alone within the bustle. Today's fast pace of living threatens this once commonplace occurrence.

"Wow, look at that table!" One neighbor boy gaped, jabbing his friend in the ribs and pointing toward our kitchen table, which was set for supper.

"That's some meal," added the other boy wistfully.

"How can they . . . ?" The younger boy paused, inquisitive yet hesitant.

"Because they are lucky, that's why," retorted the older boy.

By our standards a very simple meal awaited the family. *What was astounding about it?* I wondered. Then I realized that our table, complete with place settings for each family member and food waiting in serving dishes, was the rarity the boys were responding to. Possibly only at holidays these boys got to sit at a table that looked quite common to us. Within a year, both boys' mothers, who had found it troublesome to set the table for the family to eat together, had left their homes in search of more excitement. I have never forgotten the wistfulness in their sons' eyes as they looked at our set table.

Neither will I forget the neighbor children's enthusiasm and delight when they gathered in our backyard to sample the fresh, warm applesauce they had helped strain, or counted the soybean pods they'd plucked from one stalk. Working together is another way to enhance a spirit of contentment in our homes.

Periodically clearing clutter from closets, cupboards, and homes in general, usually adds to the feeling of contentment. Including children in this venture teaches them the value of order and gives them a sense of accomplishment.

Monitor decorating tendencies when seeking to make your home a haven of contentment. I try to ask myself, "Do I want my visitors to be impressed with my decorating or feel comfortable and content?" Which would you rather be when you visit someone's home?

Beth and her husband invited another church family to their home to share a meal. Beth's heart was warmed when the young mother called her several days later and thanked her for being content. "Your home speaks of it," she explained. "I came home feeling contented rather than fretting about what I could change or add to my home in order to keep up with the latest styles."

Do not be afraid to be content with less than the best.

For a number of years we had metal folding chairs around a used, mismatched kitchen table. The finger-prints of young children were easily washed from the chairs, and I was not distressed about small shoes scratching varnished oak. Neighbor children with dirty knees climbed onto the simple folding chairs and watched with wonder as I rolled pie dough. Those chairs, while far from stylish, helped to make my kitchen a welcome haven of contentment for youngsters.

In striving to make our homes havens of content-ment we may want to ask ourselves these questions: If Jesus visited my home, which would He compliment: the décor or the discipline? the treasures or the tone? the color schemes or evidence of eternal dreams?

Practically Speaking

Daughters of God cultivate contentment in a variety of practical ways:

- Cassandra has trained herself to limit her trips to town. Contentment and careful planning enable her to do this. Resourcefulness and more uninter-rupted days are the result, not to mention the blessing of not straining the family budget.

- Catherine has uncluttered her home in an unusual way. When they moved to their new home, she decided to "leave the pretties packed." Instead she neatly recorded Bible verses on the newly painted walls, first in pencil and then with a large marker. Her family and visitors are exposed to Scripture, and Catherine finds her housecleaning far less burdensome.

- For years, Cara lamented her large nose, promi-nent chin, and ruddy complexion. Frequently she compared her face to the attractive faces around her. Finally she repented of her discontent and reproach of her Creator. She accepted her outward appearance and focused on "the hidden man of the heart." Friends who knew her commented on how her outward appearance improved as her countenance changed, reflecting her growing inner beauty.

- Connie loves a clean house. As a farmer's wife with four young children, she has adjusted her expectations. Each week she gives several of the rooms in their large farmhouse a good cleaning. The rest of the cleaning may or may not get completed. Although her house is rarely completely clean, it is never totally dirty.

- In teaching her children contentment, Carol practices toy rotation. She has four boxes of simple but stimulating toys. For several weeks the children play with one box of toys, while the other boxes are stowed away in the attic. After several weeks have passed, the box of toys is exchanged for another one. Glad cries of "I remember this" are punctuated with laughter and play. Picking up is easier and clutter is minimized. (Hint for mothers: more and *more* toys do not make contented children.)

- Carmen strives to be thankful for the "glarrow" in her life. She recognizes the value of being content in gladness and sorrow. Even though her home was lacking in loving affirmation, she is thankful that her experiences have sensitized her to the needs of others.

Mary and Martha of Bethany are our Scriptural mentors of contentment. From their examples we learn about the value of being content in our areas of service.

Martha is sometimes accused of being out of the Lord's will. Actually, she was performing common, necessary, womanly acts of service. Her service was not wrong; her attitude and dissatisfaction were. When she complained to Jesus about Mary leaving her to serve alone, Martha was gently exhorted: "Martha, Martha, thou art careful and troubled about many things: but one thing is needful: and Mary hath chosen that good part, which shall not be taken away from her" (Luke 10:41, 42). Martha could have been content to serve without finding fault with Mary, who was serving in a different, also needful, way. Martha could also have been less concerned with her earthly duties, allowing more time for the most important—worship of her Lord.

Many women can relate to Martha. They find it difficult to lay aside their domestic duties or simply complete them with less fuss and bother. Busy Marthas can, and should, plan for some "Mary" minutes.

Blessed are the women who make time to worship their Lord with abandonment as Mary did. They may also need to learn discipline and contentment in completing the many mundane tasks of a Martha's world.

In what ways can you and I be content? What can we do less rigidly or flamboyantly in order to allow adoration time for our Saviour?

Quiet Paths

After wintering in fairer lands, my phoebe friend has returned to our neighborhood. Again her simple call encourages me. Comparing myself to others, and comparing my service to that of others, frustrates God's plans for me. I can serve Him in the ways He has called me to.

When I step away from the clutter and conveniences

of our world, I more readily hear God's affirmation and feel His smile of approval. I can hurry past cobwebbed corners and smile at sparse flower beds while I answer His bidding. I can be content without a new dress while I share the message He laid on my heart.

Daughter of God, seek His direction in your life. He will lead you — aside from the convenient, away from the clutter, beyond the comparing — to quiet paths of contentment. Worship Him there: Sometimes in temporary abandon, as Mary did when she left her domestic duties to wash Christ's feet; sometimes contentedly, serving others in the midst of your busy Martha's world.

Scriptures

"Let us therefore follow after the
things which make for peace,
and things wherewith one may edify another."
Romans 14:19

"Set your affection on things above,
not on things on the earth."
Colossians 3:2

"Let your conversation be without covetousness;
and be content with such things as ye have:
for he hath said, I will never leave thee,
nor forsake thee."
Hebrews 13:5

Prayer

Dear Heavenly Father,
   Our world scorns contentment. Your kingdom embraces it. I confess that I find myself sorely tempted to get or do more, especially when it is convenient. Far too often I compare myself to others and interfere with Your plans for my life. Forgive me, Father. Strengthen me in striving for contentment. I want to worship You, serve You, and adore You. Part of my service to You involves serving others as Martha of Bethany did. Give me wisdom. Help me not to be encumbered and ensnared in ways that prevent me from worshiping You wholeheartedly as Mary did.
   I want to be content with less so that I may do more for Thee.

Contentedly Yours,

RECEIVING
OF
GOD'S GRACE

CHAPTER 7

*Lord, I am
listening for—*

Whispers of Grace

God's grace—with all that is written and sung about it, there still remains an element of mystery to this precious gift from God. Grace is saving, enabling, empowering, and amazing. It is readily available, according to the measure of our need. We receive it simply by humbly asking for it. What a precious gift to daughters of God!

At times God's grace is shouted to us above the din of sin, drawing us to a saving or reviving faith in our Lord. At other times we experience whispers of God's grace: small affirmations of God's presence, simple confirmations of His will, or bits of comfort for a weary path. In whatever way it is bestowed, grace always strengthens us beyond our imagination.

In the Old Testament, grace was extended to a few individuals, but Jesus ushered in an abundant grace. "And the Word was made flesh, and dwelt among us, . . . full of grace and truth. For the law was given by Moses, but grace and truth came by Jesus Christ" (John 1:14, 17).

"And of his fulness have all we received, and grace for grace" (John 1:16). As daughters of God, we have all received of His grace. We experienced His saving grace when we accepted Christ as our Saviour. "Even when we were dead in sins, [God] hath quickened us together with Christ, (by grace ye are saved;) and hath raised us up together, and made us sit together in heavenly places in Christ Jesus: that in the ages to come he might shew the exceeding riches of his grace in his kindness toward us through Christ Jesus." These verses from Ephesians 2 speak not only of God's saving grace but also of the continuance of His transforming grace, vast riches from the fullness of Jesus Christ—grace heaped upon grace.

"Grace for grace": three simple words from John 1 that convey so much. While doing a word study of grace, I was captivated by this phrase which called me to delve further into its meaning. Matthew Henry's commentary lists six attributes of God's grace that this simple yet profound phrase may reveal. Daughters of God do themselves and their Lord a special favor to study grace carefully. The more we learn about grace, the more we delight in its exceeding riches and abundance! Yes, you may search, but you will never find an ending or a complete understanding of the marvelous grace of God. Amazing!

Psalm 65 speaks of God's power at work in nature. The psalmist's vivid description of God's blessing upon the earth gives a lovely word picture of God blessing us with grace. "Thou visitest the earth, and waterest it: thou greatly enrichest it with the river of God. Thou waterest the ridges thereof abundantly: thou settlest the furrows thereof: thou makest it soft with showers: thou blessest the springing thereof" (Psalm 65:9, 10). The earth springs forth with abundant crops after God has watered the ridges, settled the furrows, and sent softening showers. Likewise grace springs forth abundantly in our lives when God has blessed our steps of faith, smoothed our furrowed paths, and softened our grief by His outpouring of grace.

As children, many of us memorized definitions of grace. Do you remember rattling off a crisp explanation of grace and still not understanding what it meant? Recited definitions of grace seem simplistic and fail to capture the wonder and power of this provision. The best way to begin to *understand* grace is to *experience* it. As you read the following accounts, think of times in your own life when God has whispered grace to you.

Watered Ridges

Riveted in my mind are the details of an evening, a decade ago, when I heard a whisper of God's grace. That whisper grew into a grace that empowered me to travel on the next leg of the journey God had charted for our family.

The receding storm grumbled in the east, dragging the dark clouds away and unveiling the western sky. The last raindrops chased each other down my kitchen window, gathering momentum as each one joined the tiny rivulets that sparkled in the setting sun. As I watched, the painted sky spilled pink across the freshly bathed countryside. I grabbed the camera and followed my yearning heart outside for communion with the Creator of this panorama. Praise to my God burst from my heart as I meandered around brimming puddles. Even they reflected the brilliant blazes of pink and orange from the gleaming sunset. I stood transfixed as the splendor changed. Two distinct lines converged within the sunset so that a cross glowed more brightly than the

surrounding glory. From my vantage point, some distance out our lane, that cross was centered directly over
the family farm. As quickly as the cross had formed in
the sky, a thought burned in my mind. *Would taking up
our cross require leaving the farm? Was God giving me a
message in the midst of the splendor?* Although the
thought was troublesome, I felt a deep sense of peace.
"I will take my cross and follow; my dear Saviour I will
follow . . . ." I found myself singing the words of the
familiar hymn.

That sunset was a personal whisper of God's grace,
giving me a hint of the journey that stretched before us.
My photographs still remind me of that special glimpse
into God's leading. Now I seldom see a sunset, and
never from my kitchen window, as other homes block
our western view. The home God led us to live in is nestled in the small town where our church is located.
Through a series of events, convictions, and confirmations, my husband and I and our children did leave the
farm and picked up a cross of sorts—living in town so
that we might be a reflection of God's light in the community of our church. Born out of my husband's obedience to God's promptings are missions and ministries
for not only our family but other church families as
well. And God faithfully continues to extend grace to
us as we raise our family to embrace the principles of
God while living among people who boldly discard
them. Our testimony is that God watered the ridges
that He called us to climb. In preparing me for the ridge
ahead, God whispered His grace to me in an unusual
way that summer evening. At times when the way is
weary and the cross seems heavy, I remember that sunset, infused with the peace and presence of God, and I
am encouraged to go on by God's grace.

God asks each of us to climb ridges. We may

hesitate, wondering if we have the strength to climb and fretting about what lies beyond. Will there be other, higher ridges? deep valleys? Graciously, God waters those ridges, making the climb more pleasant. Watered ridges may be slippery at places, but the foliage is abundant and lush. Fruit and fresh drinking water are available to strengthen us as we climb. Spirits are refreshed on ridges God has watered.

God gave young Mary, the mother of His Son, whispers of His grace. Truly an honor was bestowed on her, yet the ridges ahead must have looked forbidding. God whispered a hint of His grace to her when He had Gabriel tell Mary the news of Elisabeth's expected child. God watered Mary's ridges by providing a source of spiritual refreshment to the daughter He had called to such an incredible climb. "The Magnificat," recorded in Luke 1:46-55, is Mary's testimony of God's grace to her: "My soul doth magnify the Lord, and my spirit hath rejoiced in God my Saviour."

Each daughter of God should have a collection of accounts of God's provision of grace. Journaling or testifying of these whispers of grace strengthens our faith and encourages others.

Settled Furrows

God's Word is full of graceful whispers just waiting to be found in our hour of need. In 1995 I lay, afraid and alone in a hospital bed, worrying about my premature infant in an isolette down the hall and my young children at home with my husband. Fearfully I considered my circumstances. If I succumbed to the toxins in my blood, who would care for our tiny newborn? Who would help my husband raise our children? As the IV pump pulsated rhythmically, sending protective medicine into my veins, I pulled my Bible from the bedside table and began to read. That night when I so desperately needed promises from God, I paged to a chapter where I often sought strength and comfort. From the treasures of Psalm 103 my eyes were directed to the last verses of Psalm 102. Verse 23 identified my state: "He weakened my strength in the way; he shortened my days." Words from the next verses echoed my heart's cry: "O my God, take me not away in the midst of my days." My faith was strengthened with: "Of old hast thou laid the foundation of the earth: and the heavens are the work of thy hands. They shall perish, but thou shalt endure: . . . thou art the same, and thy years shall have no end." I could rest! Regardless of the outcome of my circumstances, God would remain; He was in control. The last verse spoke a promise to my troubled soul. "The children of thy servants shall continue, and their seed shall be established before thee." I had found God's answer for me. My husband and I were serving God, and He would carefully guard our children and their souls. I could go to sleep trusting, resting in His presence.

God's plow had created fresh furrows. In my fear, I felt like our preschool son struggling across big, fresh furrows to reach his father in the distant field. But God whispered grace to me through His Word; He settled the furrows so that I could walk closely with Him. God's grace is like that. It enables us to abide in His presence, maturing in faith, when we face circumstances that evoke doubt and fear.

Today our tiny premature infant is a bubbly, active, and sensitive eleven-year-old. I recovered from the rare form of toxemia, and Holly and I joined our family at home ten days after her birth. Happily we dressed her in doll clothes and praised God for His kind care. We still rejoice and cherish those memories, but if the outcome had been different, God's great grace could still have matched our need.

Softening Showers

"My grace is sufficient for thee," God promised Paul in his struggle with a thorn in the flesh. God's grace is sufficient, especially in our hours of weakness. His whispers of grace are especially comforting during times of grief and profound need.

Joanna felt a deep sense of uneasiness even while the realization of a new life growing within thrilled her mother heart. Each of her and Harry Lee's four children eagerly anticipated the arrival of a new baby. Sixteen-year-old Kristalyn was especially excited about helping to mother another sibling. When the doctor recommended an ultrasound, Harry Lee offered to accompany Joanna. Fourteen years earlier they had buried their first son, a victim of a rare and fatal malady. He had lived only a few minutes.

After an anxious wait, Harry Lee and Joanna learned the crushing news—this baby also suffered the fatal disease. To add to their dismay, they were informed that Joanna also had a life-threatening condition. The couple was stunned when the doctor recommended an abortion. He even offered to change records so that it could be done within the parameters allowed by their state. Thus began a torturous journey for this family. Their firm resolution to value the life of their unborn child was supported by their church family and scorned by some health care professionals. Due to the risk of Joanna's life, she had to be hospitalized in a medical center some distance from their home for five long weeks. There she waited for their baby to be born — a baby whose death was certain, apart from a miracle of God. God did provide a miracle, not in the body of their unborn child but in the hearts of this daughter of God and her family.

Joanna wrote: "I dedicated those weeks to a closer relationship with God, a time of personal purification, and a treasured bonding with my baby. As we waited for the arrival of our child, it was with dread. It meant the separation from this precious life, the strain of working through grief, and the emotional mountain of a graveside service. Staying in the hospital meant separation from the family God had already given me, and it was such a strain on our children." One afternoon she felt she could take the strain no longer. She knelt by her hospital bed and pleaded with God.

At home sixteen-year-old Kristalyn was praying also. She wrote: "The days and weeks ticked by. I wanted Mom home with us but felt as though I just could not bid farewell to our precious little brother. One night I knelt beside my bed feeling exhausted and drained. 'Lord,' I prayed, 'take control. I can hardly bear the emotional strain or the workload. May Your most perfect will be accomplished soon.'" Hours after each desperate prayer was said, the time arrived and Joanna was hurried off to surgery. Their little angel lived only briefly before joining his brother in heaven. As soon as they could, the children gathered in the hospital room where the tiny form lay in the bassinet, bundled in blue. Together the family said good-bye.

Kristalyn wrote: "Tears ran like a river down my cheeks as I rocked him and held him close. It seemed so unfair that we had to say good-bye as soon as we had said hello! Each of us held him and gave him all our love.

"The following Tuesday our family, along with

many friends, stood before a small, open grave. *Must this be the result of all our prayers, hopes, dreams, and tears?* my anguished heart cried. *Just a cold grave and empty arms?* The white casket was so small to hold so much."

A sufficient grace far beyond our imagination is given to those who grieve deeply. This family received whispers of God's grace, borne to them by caring friends and family through many acts of kindness and service. During the first raw year of grieving, Harry Lee prepared a small memorial garden in their lawn. As Joanna tended the flowers they planted there, it felt as if she was pouring out her love to their little boys. It was a tangible remembrance of two lives she had longed to care for. In many ways, softening showers fell on this family's hurting hearts, preventing the hardness that the enemy wished to deposit there.

Two years later Harry Lee, Joanna, and their children were able to open their arms to another son—this one adopted from an orphanage in another country. God's grace was whispered to them again in big and small ways as they sought His direction and then stepped out in faith. They have found grace to be sufficient: strong in their hours of weakness, softening in days of temptation, *enough* for their steps of faith.

During the rewriting of this manuscript, I phoned the home of Harry Lee and Joanna to finalize permission to use their story here. Kristalyn answered. "Oh, haven't you heard our news? My parents are in China adopting a little girl!"

Grace has warmed deep grief to bloom in joy. Empty arms have found God's grace sufficient, daring to love again. Praise God for His whispers of grace to this family.

Grace Received, Grace Shared

Sandy mentally checked off the list of wedding preparations she wished to discuss with Randy. She was totally unprepared for the discussion that did take place that evening. Instead of finalizing wedding plans, Randy broke their engagement. Sandy sat stunned. Numbly she said good-bye to the man she loved.

Wedding plans stopped abruptly, except for the things that had to be undone. A partially completed wedding dress was carefully packed away amid tears and tissue paper. Each morning a feeling of dread washed over the bride that was not to be. Yet each day she experienced God's grace whispered to her in a personal way.

Then a fresh wave of grief surrounded her as stories began to leak out. On top of the rejection was the pain of rumors. With the little strength Sandy had left, she threw her cares on God and determined to extend grace to Randy. By God's grace she was able to forgive him as well as the talebearers.

Over the years, as she remained single, Sandy continued to rely on God's grace. Each time the painful memories arose, Sandy applied God's grace to them. Today this daughter of God leads a productive and happy single life, a true testimony of God's grace multiplied to her; and that grace extended to others.

For All

When, as daughters of Eve, we are overwhelmed with doubts and fears, distraught by grief, or stung by rejection, we need to cry out for the grace God lavishes on daughters of God.

What are your accounts of the whispers of God's

grace? Each daughter of God experiences His grace at her humble request and according to her need. As we receive of that grace, we are empowered with the ability to extend grace to others. It is free, so we can freely give. Never will we exhaust the supply, and what we receive will be sufficient to meet our need. Try journaling about, or testifying of, your own experiences with God's amazing grace — and so magnify the Lord!

Scriptures

"Grace and peace be multiplied unto you through the knowledge of God, and of Jesus our Lord."
2 Peter 1:2

"But unto every one of us is given grace according to the measure of the gift of Christ."
Ephesians 4:7

"That in the ages to come he might shew the exceeding riches of his grace in his kindness toward us through Christ Jesus.
For by grace are ye saved through faith; and that not of yourselves: it is the gift of God."
Ephesians 2:7, 8

Prayer

Dear God of Grace,

I am a grateful recipient of Your grace. I testify with Mary: "My soul doth magnify the Lord, and my spirit hath rejoiced in God my Saviour."

You have extended grace to me in so many ways — saving grace, enabling grace, sufficient grace. I can never thank and praise You enough for this marvelous gift.

Sometimes I feel hopeless, or helpless, or overwhelmed. During such times help me remember to ask for more grace. May I be alert for Your whispers of grace. I trust that You will water the ridges, settle the furrows, and send softening showers for my journey. As You bless me in these ways, grace will spring forth in my life and spill over into my relationships with others. In this way may I live "to the praise of the glory of [Your] grace" (Ephesians 1:6).

Listening for Whispers of Your Grace,

CHAPTER 8

Single!

Single! Or single. The difference is in the punctuation; your perspective provides the punctuation. Which are you?

Some people may consider singleness dull and un-inviting. Daughters of Eve may feel pressured to avoid it if at all possible. I am glad that many daughters of God learn to view their singleness from God's per-spective — a gracious gift! Yes, therein lies the exclama-tion point! Stanzas of a poem by Wanda Wagler express the attitude every young daughter of God should as-sume.

> To be a single person
> Is a special ministry.
> If that is what the Lord doth will
> Then naught I'd rather be.
>
> So whether God is calling me
> To singlehood or not,
> I want to follow where He leads,
> Whatever is my lot.

Yes, marriage is a glorious thing,
But so is singlehood.
I look ahead to either one
To do as Jesus would.

The Father's will brings greater joy
Than doing as I please.
So as I seek to do His will,
I'll find it on my knees.[1]
— Wanda Wagler

God has plans for your singleness. Discovering His will and adjusting your hopes and dreams for the future take time and effort. His plans may not always seem clear or fair or according to our liking, but He is God nonetheless and nothing befalls us without His permission. Acceptance of God's will, then, has a major bearing on one's perspective of singleness.

Some daughters of God gladly accept their singleness and — like the Apostle Paul — actually prefer it. Others wrestle with surrendering their desires for marriage, and consider their lot in life unfortunate. I suppose the majority of God's single daughters find themselves somewhere between the preferable claim and the unfortunate complaint. Or their perspective may vary from time to time, depending on their circumstances. When a flat tire spoils an outing, an appliance malfunctions, a dependable vehicle needs to be purchased, or one's heart longs to be cherished, having a husband looks appealing. On the other hand, if a good book begs to be read after midnight, a personal agenda tugs at one's heartstrings, or missions appeal for your service — at such times independence is valued and singlehood gleams attractively.

I asked some single friends how they feel about

being single. Here are some of their responses:

"Life as a single person is great!" wrote one. (Note the exclamation point.) She continued, "If singleness is God's will for me, I can be just as fulfilled as I would be if I were married. Singleness is *not* God's second best!"

Another wrote: "As I reflect over my single years, I am grateful for the many varied experiences and opportunities that came my way. And I praise God for His goodness and guidance through it all."

"I have so many choices right now," bubbled another friend. "Why, if I wanted to, I could be mother to needy foster children."

"God is a much better provider than a husband could ever be," notes another. "He never lets me down! There are many things I can do as a single person that I couldn't do if I were married."

"I'm not sure I like the word," one friend said. She paused, uncertain whether I would understand. I encouraged her to continue because I really wanted to hear what she had to say.

"I don't have a problem with being single, nor do I object to the word being used. But, in a way, everyone has a single life—everyone is a single person, an individual. Some of us just don't have our needs met by a spouse. Maintenance work around the house, for example. I can do some things, and I do. But it would be nice to have someone to do those things for me. And just because I do not [have a spouse], I am no less of a person."

In essence she was saying that just because she is single, she is in every way an individual and is not very different from other women. We talked about unmarried women being a minority. "So why aren't minority groups people?" she asked. Of course, in reality we all know they are people, but her question and her comments helped me realize that sometimes unmarried daughters of Eve wish to be treated and addressed as individuals rather than as "singles." Could it be that our identities as married women are so infiltrated by our husbands and children that we somehow view an unmarried sister in the church as less than complete? If so, we stand to be corrected.

The ideas expressed by this friend were not isolated sentiments. They were echoed in the comments of others.

"Just because I'm single, doesn't mean I am not a complete person. I'm still important, and it is okay to have an agenda of my own. Of course that all needs to be in reason — I need to be willing to be flexible too."

"I do not care to be referred to as 'an unclaimed blessing.' I can be a blessing as a single person."

"Did I miss the boat? No. Or if I did, fine. God knows what is my best transportation through life."[2]

After sixty-plus years of single life, one of my single friends married a widower. In a letter to friends she wrote:

"It is now three months since we were married. Our wedding day was one of the most beautiful days of my life, and the memories will always be with me. It is certainly a good life and is enriched as we grow in our new life together. But I also cherish my single years, and will always have a special respect for my single friends."

Of interest to me was that she called her wedding day *one* of the most beautiful days of her life—not *the* most beautiful day, just one of them. I am fully confident that this daughter of God would have been

114

perfectly content to remain single until death. God's plan surprised her, but she is delighting in it as she delighted in her many single years.

Regardless of how much one enjoys being single, living alone has its challenges and requires surrender. Just as a married daughter of God surrenders to God's will and her husband's leadership, so a single daughter of God surrenders to God's will for her life and accepts her role as a single woman.

Role Taking

What is the role of the single woman? Where does she fit into the church and community? Singles I know share that sometimes they struggle with assuming a role of which they feel uncertain. For instance, when is a single woman considered an adult rather than a youth? Where is her place in the church? How can she expect to be treated?

Rita writes:

"Around 23 or 24 years of age I sensed a need for recognition and treatment as an adult and not as a youth and potential prospect for marriage. People asked my age and responded, 'Oh, you are young yet; you still might find that special someone.' Inwardly a pang of hurt and frustration evolved. Why was I looked at as a *youth* and a *prospect*? When inquiring about my age, why did they not ask questions about what I do or plan to do with my life?"

Some of the frustration results from the confusion of others in regard to the single person's identity. Why do some church ushers, for instance, insist that single women sit in the youth section during special church services? One single sister related how it seemed to be marital status rather than age that accounted for where she was directed to sit. "If I had a man walking beside me or a little baby in my arms, no questions would be asked or pressure put upon me to sit in the specified youth section, even if I were only seventeen years of age." Or consider the plight of a single woman who moved from a youth Sunday school class to an adult class and struggled to feel accepted.

Our role as fellow church members is to make unmarried daughters of God feel accepted and needed in our congregations. Many of them play important, supportive roles in the church. Frequently they are involved in child care or instruction. Their gifts of hospitality and congeniality are an asset to other believers and guests alike.

Recently I attended a mother-daughter supper at another church. Nearly sixty mothers and daughters gathered to share an evening of fellowship. Included in the number were several women from the community who were attending the church or had befriended its members. All were delighted by the pleasantly decorated tables and fruit trays. Gardening was the theme of the evening, with speakers sharing how sowing, cultivating, and harvesting relate to the Christian life. At each place setting was a tiny ceramic flowerpot with a sprig of ivy beginning to grow—a gift to the woman or child who sat there. Behind the scenes was a very happy single woman who had thoroughly enjoyed the planning, decorating, and breaking off sprigs of her ivy plants to start in the tiny pots she had found "on sale for only twenty-five cents each!" Other women shared the responsibility of preparing the food, but Kayleen had spent many hours doing things for the enjoyment and relaxation of other women. And she had done it willingly. Her cheer and attention to detail made the evening especially pleasant. The women in that congregation expressed gratitude for her willingness to share her talents; at the same time Kayleen was rewarded with a sense of fulfillment in caring for others.

If confused about her role in life, an unmarried woman can step out in confidence and assume a role. I know single women happily serving God as nurses or nurse's aides, teachers or teacher's aides, foster mothers, nannies, secretaries, housekeepers, writers, and missionaries. Their presence and abilities are welcomed in our churches. Never are they denied the privilege of being daughters of God.

Acceptance Please

Married adults convey acceptance to the singles in church in a variety of ways. Inviting them into our homes for a visit and a meal is especially appreciated. Including them in our conversations, group activities, and community outreach communicates not only acceptance but also personal value.

Singles themselves play an important part in their acceptance by others. Kelly writes: "A single person needs to be careful of her attitude. Don't take offense at what married people do and say. Look for the best motives."

Rita acknowledges that she needed to deal with her irritations regarding less than respectful treatment. Talking about her feelings, crying, and singing defused her frustrations; but examining her position in Christ brought even more victory. She writes:

"As for my position in Christ, I learned — and am still learning — that people's intentional or unintentional mistreatments do not and cannot lower my position in Christ or nullify my worth to Jesus. I had to come

117

face-to-face with this truth to avoid self-pity and anger."

Rita took steps to assimilate the truth of her position in Christ. First, she focused on God's goodness to her. Second, she sometimes shared with the "mistreatment givers" how it felt to be treated in such a way. To her encouragement, some of them were eager to correct their mistakes. Third, she avoided some places where she frequently encountered awkward situations or | unjust treatment. Last, she invited married couples into her home for a meal. The time of visiting helped them understand each other better.

Have you noticed how single women enjoy each other's company? Our congregation is blessed with a fair number of unmarried women. They are frequently planning or doing such delightful things: going to a cabin for a weekend, surprising each other for their birthdays, hiking mountain trails, meeting together to work on hobbies, visiting widows or invalids—the list goes on. It is not unusual to see a few of them gathered in serious conversation, or a group of them laughing heartily at the latest birthday surprise. In no way do I get the impression that life has passed them by—and indeed it has not. They are assuming another important role of the unmarried: to support each other and enjoy togetherness.

Reaching Out

Serving the Lord by reaching out to others electrifies singlehood. According to the Apostle Paul in 1 Corinthians 7:34, this is one of the rich benefits of not caring for a spouse. Reaching out to serve others most often fulfills an unmarried daughter of God in her desire to be useful and nurturing. Rebecca writes:

118

"My nursing career has been a real blessing to me in my singlehood. It provides purpose and a satisfaction to be able to help someone. To feel needed is one of the basic needs of all mankind, and nursing fulfilled that need in my life. Also, working on the mission field and in voluntary service units was a way of reaching out that helped me find and fill my place in life. Working in midwifery in other countries was a means of demon- strating my love for infants and children."

A relative of hers told me recently that Rebecca delivered over six hundred babies. After spending nearly forty fulfilling years of reaching out to others, Rebecca now finds joy in being the wife of a widower.

Nina voices her former frustration in seeking friend- ships: "At one time I was discouraged with the older women at church, wondering why they didn't reach out to me. Scripture says the older women are to teach the younger women. I wondered why they weren't fulfill- ing their duty." She went on to explain how she learned to reach out to them. "Sometimes I went to a bulk-food store and bought oatmeal, peanut butter, and chocolate chips in large quantities. Then I'd bake dozens of mon- ster cookies, put them into plastic buckets, and give them to the ladies from church." Nina's method of reaching out was successful. Soon she enjoyed a com- fortable relationship with many of the older women. They became some of her dearest friends and strongest supporters. When she went to another country to serve in voluntary service, her faithful, older friends show- ered her with letters of encouragement. Nina's wisdom and willingness to share were a blessing to me, and I presumed she had absorbed at least a portion of that wisdom from the older friends whose friendship and mentoring she carefully (and tastefully) sought.

Single or married, if you want to drown thoughts of

self-pity, or silence thoughts of self-condemnation, or rest within the strong tower of God's will—reach out!

Other Challenges

Finding acceptance and a sense of identity while experiencing fulfillment in life is not the only challenge facing unmarried daughters of God.

"What do you see as some of the greatest challenges of single life?" I asked several friends. They mentioned the following:

- Being able to rest in God's future for me. "Who will care for me when I am old?" queried Marcy. "Sometimes making a living and providing for myself becomes a burden. Then I worry about the future. It would feel nice to be able to depend on someone."

- Finding God as my strength rather than seeking strength in others. "I went to other people with my problems sooner than I went to God," lamented Nina. "I've changed though. Now I go to God first. Sometimes I still talk to a close friend or older woman, but I've also learned to rely on God rather than solely on others."

- Waiting for the right partner, if I am to have a partner. "The older I got, the more tempted I was to marry someone who I knew would marry me, but who I knew would disappoint me," said one single woman. Others acknowledged that at times they were tempted to lower their standards to acquire a husband. Waiting and standing true to convictions were rewarded with peace and satisfaction.

- Maintaining purity. Some singles find this a

greater challenge than do others. Claiming Isaiah 54:5 "For thy Maker is thine husband; the LORD of hosts is his name," and putting on the whole armor of God (Ephesians 6:14-18) strengthens daughters of God for the battle with the flesh.

- Wanting companionship. "At first I tried to seek companionship with boys or men," remembers one insightful young lady. "But then I realized I was going to the wrong source. I began actively seeking friendship with, and mentoring from, older women. These women became some of my best friends."

- Wanting a family of my own. "As I grew closer to midlife," related Rose, "I felt a desperate urge to have a family and cuddle a baby of my own." She knew time was running out for her desire to be fulfilled, but as she submitted to God's will and surrendered her desires, God provided her with a job working directly with young children. With joy she cuddled and nurtured to her heart's content.

- Taking care of my attitude. Iris spoke of her struggle with unhealthy attitudes toward those who labeled her "single" while seeming to ignore her individuality. "Just because we are single doesn't mean we aren't people with thoughts and feelings that need to be considered."

- Getting jobs done around the house that usually a man would do. Some single women have become capable do-it-yourselfers. They tackle plugged spouting, clogged plumbing, leaking faucets, full mousetraps, oil changes, and flat tires. Some of them even smile about their acquired expertise. Others have fathers or brothers who do the jobs they find overwhelming. Still others have be-friended church families who help them do main-tenance and repairs. "It is amazing how God supplies my needs, sometimes even before I am aware of them," rejoiced Kayleen after some coworkers noticed and helped her replace worn tires.

Committed Steps

Unmarried women are really not so different from married women. Indeed many married women have wrestled with the above challenges as well. We share in being daughters of Eve, with desires and struggles typical of women. The similarities that unite us are greater than the differences — and they certainly do not need to divide us.

All of us are encouraged by those who are single! We appreciate their committed steps in God's will. I thrill when I see a woman do as Ruth the Moabitess did. She took committed steps despite her disappointments. She willingly embraced God without the promise of a hus-band. "Intreat me not to leave thee, or to return from following after thee: for whither thou goest, I will go; and where thou lodgest, I will lodge: thy people shall be my people, and thy God my God" (Ruth 1:16). Her famous words, though sometimes sung at weddings, were spoken to another woman, her mother-in-law, while Ruth set one committed foot before the other in her search for God.

Mary, too, gives us an example of commitment to the plan of God. Even though she was betrothed, or engaged, she was single when the angel announced that she would mother God's Son. Although we cannot be certain of the chain of events, it is entirely possible that Mary left Nazareth and traveled to her cousin Elisabeth's house without speaking to Joseph of the miraculous conception. When she returned over three months later she was "found with child," and Joseph was "minded to put her away [secretly]" (Matthew 1:18, 19). Mary was willing to risk losing her relationship with Joseph in order to carry out God's will. What daughter of God cannot be challenged by that level of commitment?

Mary Magdalene, the first woman to see our Lord after His Resurrection, may well have been unmarried. Christ had dramatically changed her life; and this woman, along with others, was faithful in "ministering unto him" at the time of His death (Matthew 27:55, 56). God blessed her in a special way: "Now when Jesus was risen early . . . he appeared first to Mary Magdalene, out of whom he had cast seven devils" (Mark 16:9). At risk of being doubted (and she was), "she went and told them that had been with him, as they mourned and wept" (verse 10). For a time on that unsurpassed morning, Mary Magdalene was the only one who knew for certain that the believers' grief would change to joy.

What challenges to unmarried women of every age: embrace God with or without the promise of a husband. Surrender to the Lord's will even if it may cost you greatly. Serve the Lord wholeheartedly and unwaveringly. Tell others what you have found — a living, personal Saviour. He will become most precious to you. He really can be the only husband you will ever need.

Unmarried daughter of God, I echo this salutation: "Simon Peter, a servant and an apostle of Jesus Christ, to them that have obtained like precious faith with us through the righteousness of God and our Saviour Jesus Christ: grace and peace be multiplied unto you through the knowledge of God, and of Jesus our Lord, according as his divine power hath given unto us all things that pertain unto life and godliness, through the knowledge of him that hath called us to glory and virtue: whereby are given unto us exceeding great and precious promises: that by these ye might be partakers of the divine nature, having escaped the corruption that is in the world through lust" (2 Peter 1:1-4).

God has a place, and a role, for each of His daughters. My friend Lucy says it so well:

"Known unto God," James told the Jerusalem conference, "are all his works from the beginning of the world." I believe that means God knew from the moment I entered the world whether I would marry or not. He has the map of His kingdom laid out like a giant puzzle. Each of us is one of those puzzle pieces with a distinct role to fill. God knows where each of us fits the minute He picks us from the pile of pieces, the moment He forms us from the dust.

"For many of those niches in the puzzle, He needs a married man or woman to carry out His plan to 'be fruitful, and multiply, and replenish the earth.' But some corners require specially fitted pieces. God needs devoted, single Christians to fill those places."[2]

Single? Do not disregard your wondrous opportunity to glory in an intimate relationship with your Father, God! And don't delete the exclamation point!

Scriptures

"There is difference also between a wife and a virgin.
The unmarried woman careth
for the things of the Lord,
that she may be holy both in body and in spirit:
but she that is married careth
for the things of the world,
how she may please her husband."
1 Corinthians 7:34

"And this I speak for your own profit;
not that I may cast a snare upon you,
but for that which is comely,
and that ye may attend upon
the Lord without distraction."
1 Corinthians 7:35

"I will love thee, O LORD, my strength.
The LORD is my rock, and my fortress,
and my deliverer;
my God, my strength, in whom I will trust;
my buckler, and the horn of my salvation,
and my high tower."
Psalm 18:1, 2

Prayer

Written by Kayleen, a single friend.

Dear Heavenly Father,

*What a special privilege it is to know that I am Your treasured daughter! I know that in You alone I can find complete acceptance and an endless supply of love. Still at times the hurt is there — no man has chosen me as his special beloved one. But **You** have chosen me, and Your plan is best. Father, I choose to follow it with joy. Help me to use my time to serve You by serving others. Don't let me waste the gift of singleness that You have entrusted to me. Thank You for Your limitless grace for every day!*

Your Cherished Child,

_____

CHAPTER 9

Blessing Bows and Painting Pictures

I suppose every young daughter of Eve does as I did. I observed the marriages in my world and thought about what I wanted to copy and what I wanted to change if I had the opportunity to marry. As a daughter of God, I wanted my marriage to glorify Him. Highest on my list of priorities was the commitment to marry a godly man, one who would provide spiritual leadership in our home. Like many young brides-to-be, my expectations ballooned unrealistically. Ideals teetered under testing and another starry-eyed wife learned that marriage is hard — but rewarding — work.

Cording Bows

As unto the bow the cord is,
So unto the man is woman;
Though she bends him, she obeys him,
Though she draws him, yet she follows;
Useless each without the other![1]

The above lines are tucked in the middle of Henry Wadsworth Longfellow's ballad, "The Song of Hiawatha." They arrested my attention in literature class. As a teenage girl, I found myself fascinated by this poetic description of marriage. I had learned the fundamentals of carefully bending a bow to attach the cord and then pulling back on the cord to propel an arrow from the bow toward its mark. Hoping to someday understand more of the mystery of marriage, I never forgot Longfellow's captivating analogy. It illustrates the beautiful balance that may be attained in marriage; for in marrying a woman, a man is drawn by her and allows himself to be bent like a bow for the attaching of the cord. He leaves selfish ambitions and parents in order to provide and care for his wife. And though she has drawn him, a wife follows her husband. While she has bent him, she obeys him. A cord keeps a bow bent, but it is tied to both ends of the bow in complete submission. In marrying a man, a woman commits herself to a place of submission. In many ways her life is "tied" to the man she pledges to love. This delicate balance and union was God's idea, and He performed the first marriage. "Therefore shall a man leave his father and his mother, and shall cleave unto his wife: and they shall be one flesh" (Genesis 2:24).

The bow and cord analogy continues to challenge me in my relationship with my husband. *Do I work with or against my bow? Am I taut and true? Do I twang in ready submission? Do we function as a team in sending forth arrows?*

When a bow is bent and the cord attached, a useful tool is created, one that is unified and functional, ready to shoot arrows. Neither the bow nor the cord can accomplish alone what they can achieve when bound together. So also the bending of a man and the submitting of a woman create a union that is well designed to produce offspring and release them into the future. "As arrows are in the hand of a mighty man; so are children of the youth. Happy is the man that hath his quiver full of them" (Psalm 127:4, 5).

Our Archer, God, delights in using balanced bows.

Painting the Picture

Marriage was not designed for procreation only. The union is holy in that it represents Christ's love for believers. In writing to husbands and wives about their obligations, Paul states in Ephesians 5:32, 33: "This is a great mystery: but I speak concerning Christ and the church. Nevertheless let every one of you in particular so love his wife even as himself; and the wife see that she reverence her husband." Think of the serious responsibility and the glorious privilege of displaying the love of Christ Jesus for the church. Our marriages are meant to paint a picture of that profound love.

As a young child I watched with avid interest as my sister mixed oil paints on a palette and brushed them onto canvas. I remember the feeling of anticipation as I watched an image or a scene emerge beneath her careful brush strokes. But before the interesting colors and shapes took form, my sister did what I considered mundane preparation. First, she stretched and stapled the canvas over a wooden frame. Then she painted the canvas pure white with a foundation paint. And always there were times of waiting while the paint dried.

Before a Christian couple marries and begins painting a picture of Christ's love, they should be stretched into God's will and conformed to His timing. Their painting will emerge most beautiful if it is begun on a foundation of purity. Both husband and wife wield brushes—the painting is produced through teamwork. Brush strokes may be hesitant or faltering, but they can be blended or allowed to dry so that mistakes may be painted over.

Even the best artists repaint and touch up their paintings. They stand at a distance and evaluate their work. Some scrutinize the canvas upside down or in a mirror. Always they critically examine whether the right message is portrayed. We should critique our marriages with the same care, using the Bible as a mirror and defining guide. Crises of life capsize our canvas at times, providing us with an inverted view. And always there are times of waiting while newly-learned lessons dry into lasting, pleasing brush strokes.

I shudder to think what may have happened if I had picked up a brush and tried to help my older sister paint on a canvas that was to be presented to her art instructor. But in marriage both my husband and I are expected to paint together—a work of art to be presented to the world, a labor of love to represent Christ.

I like to find word pictures to help me understand and rise to the task at hand. Join me in comparing these two descriptive analogies to Scriptural truths about marriage. While we cannot in one chapter give comprehensive archery and art courses, we can examine characteristics of a fine bow and cord, and we can practice a few brush strokes that will improve our paintings. Each of us can inspect our relationship with our spouse. We can evaluate the message we are sending to the world.

Just as the devil tempted Eve, he continues to tempt daughters of Eve to rely on their own powers and yield to their own desires. Daughters of God remember that their desires have been sanctified and redirected. They are willing to crucify their own desires and to submit to

God who has promised to fulfill the desires of those who delight in Him.

Christ bent in divine love, shedding His blood and giving His life for His wife — for me, for you — and for all believers. As His bride we are called to yield to the lordship of Christ in complete submission. God bent toward us; we submit to Him. The resulting mystical union will one day culminate in a divine marriage that will last for eternity. What glory! Determine to convey this message on the canvas of your marriage.

Daughter of God—Your Part in Painting for His Glory

Prepare your canvas carefully. Allow yourself to be stretched to God's will. Paint your canvas with the white paint of a pure relationship with God and your spouse.

Begin your work of art with love and respect. By God's grace, you will have years to work on the details. Here are thirteen brush strokes that will help us paint for His glory.

1. Accepting my Honorable Occupation

Consider your honorable occupation. Proverbs 18:22 says: "Whoso findeth a wife findeth a good thing, and obtaineth favour of the LORD." Did your husband find a good thing when he found you? Did my husband experience the favor of God when he married me? Am I an advantageous gift from God to my husband? Are you? God considers ours an honorable occupation. Do we treat it as such? Do we delight in bending and submitting to our bows?

Years ago I visited a home where the wife was especially critical and condescending. As I talked with the couple, I was astounded to realize that the husband was not able to say one thing that his wife did not challenge, correct, or argue about. Time and again the man fell silent, but his rocking chair rocked a bit harder and the muscles of his jaw flexed. I had to wonder if that jaw wished to talk but was biting his tongue instead! I found myself trying to put the man at ease by complimenting his remarks.

Certainly this wife was not being a helpful gift from God. After many years of marriage this couple was still caught in detrimental ways of communicating. The wife, instead of building up her husband, continually tore him down. From the way his rocking chair pulsated against the floor I wondered if this "bow" was near breaking. The husband, who was supposed to be leading his wife, was not directing her away from disrespect. His "cord" snapped and sizzled with damaging power. What a polluted picture of marriage they painted for their offspring and acquaintances. How different things might have been if this wife had learned to be prudent.

2. Prizing Prudence

Proverbs 19:14 states, "A prudent wife is from the Lord." A prudent wife is careful to avoid errors; she is wise and discreet, especially in dealing with others. A prudent wife examines herself and her relationship with her husband. When she becomes aware of ways she disgruntles or disgraces her husband, she repents and chooses to be prudent. When a wife refuses to evaluate her own behavior and is constantly critical of her husband, she negates her purpose in married life and often becomes contentious. As daughters of God, we know we are not to be contentious, and when we are, we are compared to a constant dripping of water — an annoyance. "Contentious" simply means *quarrelsome.*

Ask yourself these questions: *Do I often quarrel with my husband? Do I frequently correct my husband? Do I do it in front of others? Am I obstinate, unyielding, and inflexible?* Sometimes we overlook or excuse our faults. Do we have the courage to ask our husbands these questions about ourselves? Will my husband have the courage to answer them honestly? Will I counter his answer? ("You can't say that!" "I am not . . .") Will I choose to strive for prudence?

Contentiousness certainly counters the honorable occupation God has called us to. What kind of wife do you and I desire to be?

 ### 3. *Allowing Desire to Be Directed*

"Thy desire shall be to thy husband." These words thrill the new bride, concern the mature wife, agitate the controlling wife, confuse the unequally yoked wife, and confound the world. We are not uncomfortable with the desiring, but rather the specific direction of our desire — "to thy husband, and he shall rule over thee" (Genesis 3:16). Not only do we squirm, at times, about our desire being toward our husbands, but we may also react to being ruled over.

Today society resists rule. Feminists demand their "rights" and seek power and control, believing they are escaping oppression and a place of inferiority. Deceived by this movement, many women scorn and reject a life of submission, completely missing the blessing and protection God ordained for them. Desires continue to be strong, but direction of those desires and submission to rule are rejected and obliterated. Little wonder that some men have responded in anger, disrespect, or stubborn passivity. If leadership is rejected, why lead?

Desire was strongly evident in the first woman, Eve. When tempted in the Garden of Eden, her desire was toward the tree (pleasant to the eye), toward the fruit (pleasant to the taste), and toward the fruit of the fruit (wisdom—pleasant to the mind). Eve's desire snagged her and led her into sin.

Gone was the tranquility of their garden home. Today we are still plagued by the struggle for men to lead and women to submit. God calls for obedience to the guiding principles He knows are safest for us. Why do we resist them?

If you are a married woman, your natural desire is toward your husband—or at least it was at one time. You have longed after him, desired his love, his understanding, his care and protection. As a Christian wife you have desired his spiritual leadership. You have undoubtedly experienced frustration when your desires have not been met to your level of expectation. What do we as daughters of God do when this is the case? Do we insist that our desires be met? Do we seek other sources to meet our desires? Do we deny or stifle our desires? God created us with desires, and He has provided direction for us. Might we try adjusting our expectations?

4. Adjusting Expectations

"Why should I change my expectations?" you may ask. "Why can't he raise his level of commitment?" "Why can't he fulfill my desires?" Valid questions, wrong assumption. Assuming that our husbands need to change while we stubbornly plow along in our own protected ruts makes us unpleasant traveling companions! What husband wants a wife nagging him to improve while she continues to wallow in self-pity?

"But he *needs* to change," you may wail. True; there are ways in which every husband could change for the better. (For that matter, what wife is beyond improvement?) The problem lies in accepting just *who* is to effect that change. *God* is in the business of changing lives. *We* have been asked by God to submit to, rather than change, this man. Remember the bow and cord. Your husband bent for you. Are you going to try so hard to change him that you break him and render the once strong, arched wood useless?

I blush when I remember my early attempts to change my husband. Praise God for His mercy; faithfully He worked on me until I saw the error of my ways. After I repented, God gently refined me. The process hurt and humbled, but I am so grateful God arrested my attention and directed my desire before I strained my handsome bow to the breaking point.

In my deep desire to fill the void of a godly man to lead in my life, I expected my husband to fulfill all my desires and meet my spiritual needs. I had to learn a basic truth about marriage: No husband will ever meet *all* his wife's needs or fulfill *all* her desires. (If our husbands would meet all our needs, we would cease to feel the need of God. Furthermore, what we view as "needs" are usually only strong desires—and yes, they may be God-given, righteous desires—that really can be met by God, rather than exclusively by our husbands.)

Only God can meet our deepest desires. Or He may decide to change our desires, or leave them unmet—at least to our level of expectation. He may use husbands or other people to meet some desires, but no human is equipped to meet all the desires of another human. If a bride expects marriage to completely fulfill her desires, her balloons of expectation will burst.

By God's grace, I learned to do two very important things. First, I turned to God with my needs and un-fulfilled desires, claiming Psalm 37:4: "Delight thyself also in the LORD; and he shall give thee the desires of thine heart." I redirected my desire toward the Lord; I purposed to delight Him. And as I did, I also delighted in met desires. It was during those years that I began to focus on the blessedness of being a daughter of God. I did not deny the dearth of godly men in my early life. Nor did I stifle my desire for a strong, godly leader. I did not give up hope that my husband would be strengthened in spiritual leadership. I did allow God to comfort and encourage me.

The second thing I learned was to adjust my expec-tations. I thank God for the older, wiser woman who came alongside me after I had confided in her. She helped me see that I was married to a strong, godly man; he just led differently than I thought he should. I expected my husband to change without considering how I needed to change. Gradually I deflated my ex-pectations and released the tight grip on my bow. I praised my husband for the positives about his leader-ship, and I relaxed in his leadership rather than trying to improve it or bend it to my specifications. Unified in a more balanced way, we were able to help each other grow in spiritual maturity. My bow bent with comfort, I submitted to him with new ease, and now our Archer uses us both to send forth arrows for His service.

Do I expect perfection? Are we always united as a balanced bow and cord? Do I no longer struggle with the urge to pull tightly on my bow? Does my husband fulfill all my desires? The answers are all no. I *adjusted my expectations*, remember?

As I adjusted and changed, my husband also changed. I didn't need to change him; God did. I now experience the fulfillment of my deepest desires, and my husband has become an even stronger godly leader in our home.

 ### 5. Changing: *Know That He Will Never Be the Same*

Having emphasized that a wife is not to change her husband, I will now tell you a secret every woman should know: You cannot change your husband, and yet—because of you—he will never be the same. You cannot change him because change comes about in one's life by the work of God and the cooperation of that individual. However, because your husband has loved you and received your love, felt your admiration, coveted your respect, cringed at your criticism, prayed for your growth, calmed your fears, confronted your doubts, fathered your children, and listened to your heart—for all the many ways he has or has not connected with you—he will never be the same. You have had a profound effect on the life of your husband. In these ways you have altered his character without trying to change the man.

The gray-haired couple caught my attention as they sat among a group of ministers at a conference. The tender way he looked down at her while conversing and the sweetness with which she returned his gaze in affirmation was touching. I found myself wondering about their relationship. Later, I had the rich treasure of being with this woman in a small prayer group. It was from her that I learned the dynamics of changing myself or my husband. Here was an elderly wife excited about what God had done in her life. I still remember how she told another young wife and me how she had prayed for years for her husband to change. Although he was a minister, she felt they rarely communicated on a spiritual level. "I tried so hard to change him into the man I thought he should be," she said with a sad shake of her head. Then a smile spread across her face as she continued. "And then one day I saw clearly how I needed to change. I prayed that God would change me into the person He wanted me to be." Here her expressive, wrinkled face grimaced. "Oh, how God worked on me. He *really* worked on me!" With awe she said, "And as I changed, my husband changed. He became a tender man who shared spiritual insights with me in the way I had longed for him to do."

That dear saint then prayed a prayer of blessing and encouragement on the other young wife and me as we joined in prayer.

Given their ages at the time I met this charming couple, I assume they may now be in glory. I do not even remember their names, but that woman's testimony, enhanced by the peaceful delight of her countenance, held valuable lessons for me. I thank God for her honesty and her courage to mentor me.

Take heart, Daughter of God, balance and unity *are* possible when you are bound to your husband—even one in need of change. Are you guaranteed that your husband will change if you do? Probably he will. Change because you want to change—for God, not so that you can be certain to effect change in your husband's life. "Create in me a clean heart, O God; and renew a right spirit within me" (Psalm 51:10). Too often it is easier to pray: Create in *him* a clean heart, O God . . .

6. Asking: Am I Tight, Twiddling, or Taut?

Before you congratulate yourself on not being a tight cord, not trying to control your bow, let me issue another word of caution. A tight cord is not the only problem a bow may experience. A loose bowstring also renders a bow ineffective. A lax cord does not rebound in following the bow when it is drawn back for shooting. Nor does it keep the bow bent to the degree that makes an effective union between the bow and the cord. The vibrant "twang" that should issue from a taut cord is reduced to a dull "flop" as the loose bowstring returns to a passive position. Twiddling, the cord may need to be untangled before it can be drawn back in readiness.

How may a wife be like a loose bowstring? Exchanging tautness for twiddling may indicate that a woman is too busy with trifles. Think about it. Do things of importance keep us at rapt attention? Or do we twirl around the trivial?

A woman who is passively subordinate to the point that she never voices her opinions or appeals her husband's decisions may be likened to a loose cord. One husband said: "I dislike when my wife is like a limp dishrag without opinions to share with me." In contrast, the decisively submissive wife has *chosen* to submit after honest evaluation and expression.

What value is there in expressing my thoughts and feelings? Why should I even consider making an appeal? Because a taut cord exerts just the right amount of pressure to effectively bend a bow. A taut cord draws the bow and yet it submits. It zings quickly into place behind the bow in a beautiful, effective submission. Determine today to exchange your tight grip or your loose droopiness for a tender tautness. Then watch God bless your finely corded bow.

7. Teaching Him to Love

"Husbands, love your wives, even as Christ also loved the church, and gave himself for it; that he might sanctify and cleanse it with the washing of water by the word" (Ephesians 5:25, 26). How does a husband really love his wife if he is unaware of her innermost desires or struggles? By sharing on a personal level, a wife may teach her husband how to love her more. By being vulnerable and transparent, a wife allows a husband glimpses into her soul and calls forth his spiritual guidance. He is then better able to "cleanse her" by washing her with the refreshing water of God's Word. What Christian wife does not long for that kind of love?

God created women with feelings and perspectives quite different from those of men. He does not ask married women to squelch their doubts, fears, and godly desires to the degree that their husbands do not have the opportunity to learn from them. A demanding, insensitive man may have a loose cord flopping passively behind him, a woman who has not had the courage to teach him how to love her.

An important interjection here: Some women have attempted this kind of communication only to be laughed to scorn or ordered to submit by a husband who has not been tenderized to the weaker vessel. In cases such as this it is easy for a woman to close herself off and not express her true feelings for fear she will be rebuffed. In so doing she does not encourage her husband to bend toward her in love. The spiritual leadership she desires may also remain dormant. In my observation, couples who grow old in this type of union tend to be insensitive to each other and those around them; their focus leans toward surface issues rather than deeper, spiritual truths. Painting a picture of

Christ's love for the church in this way clouds the deepest, truest hues.

Sometimes men do not respond favorably to their wives' attempts to tenderly teach them about love. In reality there are times when no matter how hard a wife tries, her husband continues to smear the painting with big blotches of mismatched paint. (Wives can do the same.) In these cases God's grace is available and sufficient to meet needs and desires. God did not remove Paul's thorn in the flesh, and He may choose not to remove yours. (Remember, He does not force His children to change.) Take courage. Your marriage may not paint an attractive picture of God's love, but your life and your responses can paint a picture of God's grace and His marvelous redemption. God may intend to use the circumstances of your life to minister to or mentor others in a remarkable way. Or He may choose to one day "restore to you the years that the locust hath eaten" (Joel 2:25). Chapter 10 will acquaint you with women who paint alone or add bright brush strokes to darkened canvases.

 8. Teaching Tenderly

In delicate balance, a godly wife can become a tender teacher for her husband. Women are often naturally aware of how to tenderly teach children. Wives sometimes need to learn that they can also tenderly teach their husbands if they are careful to do it respectfully. A wife can tenderize her husband toward her own longings and desires as well as toward the care of others. (Many nurturing mothers have taught sons or husbands how to tenderly hold and care for infants and children.)

A woman's tears may teach a husband much about

her passions and personality. Or a woman's fears may balance a husband's sense of adventure. By sharing from the depths of her soul, she can teach her husband about a woman's inner beauty, a treasure of the weaker vessel.

How does one become a tender teacher? First, ask God to help you and then expand your vision. Rather than just identifying and complaining (or nagging) about your husband's problem areas, look for ways to help him.

I appreciate the testimony of a woman who tenderly taught her husband to pray aloud for her when she was distressed or sad. First, she began praying prayers of blessing and courage into his ear at times when she was aware of his struggles. After she taught him to receive that blessing, she then gathered courage and asked him to pray aloud for her when she was disheartened. This wife often encouraged her husband by telling him how much his prayers meant to her, and she purposed to trust him even when she felt afraid to do so. Her tender teaching evoked tender treatment and spiritual care from her husband.

There is not a simple six-step method of becoming a tender teacher to your husband. Study your husband, his likes and dislikes, his strengths and weaknesses. Together you and the Lord can determine just what blend of talking, tears, quiet confidence, humor, honor, or other teaching tools you may use to bend your bow. And remember, "Though she bends him, she obeys him." The goal of teaching is not to escape obedience. Be certain to honor God and respect your husband. Do not assume an attitude of superiority. The Bible restricts a woman's teaching in public and commands her not "to usurp authority over the man" (1 Timothy 2:12). Tender teachers will not teach disrespectfully. They refrain from teaching authoritatively or in front of others. They do not use tears or tantrums to get their own way. Have you seen women bend their husbands toward them emotionally only to coerce them into fulfilling their materialistic desires and break the family financially? We need to mind our motives and tenderly teach with our husbands' best interests at heart.

A wife who has taken time to learn the fine art of being a tender teacher will truly be the best comrade a husband has.

 ## 9. Saying No to Nagging

How much harder it is for a man to follow God's command to love his wife as his own body if she is a nagging wife. Nagging is a disrespectful way of reminding someone of his failures or shortcomings. Husbands differ in their definitions of nagging. Some appreciate gentle reminders. A few may accept more than one reminder. Some prefer a list of jobs to be done around the house. But no husband appreciates sarcastic, disrespectful reminders or "To Do" lists with wife-appointed and controlled deadlines!

Whatever irritates you or tempts you to nag—disregard for spiritual things, incomplete home improvements, disorganized tools, paper clutter, or even something as simple as uncapped toothpaste tubes—decide to extend grace and forgiveness to your husband. Yes, there will be times when our husbands seem to *need* nagging. Have you heard wives say, or been tempted to say yourself, "It will not get done if I don't nag!"? Determine rather to mention a matter once or twice (according to your husband's preference) and then talk to God about the problem. Or you may change from disrespectful nagging to graceful appealing.

10. Appealing Gracefully

I had to learn to appeal. After hearing an older wife speak about the value of appealing, I headed to my dictionary for direction: "An earnest entreaty for aid, sympathy, or the like. A supplication." Rolling the definition around in my mind I realized that the concept was Scriptural and the very root of prayer. During my devotional time I found an example of women making an appeal to their authorities.

In Numbers 27:1-11 the daughters of Zelophehad approached Moses, Eleazar the priest, and leaders of the assembly with a request. "Why should the name of our father be done away from among his family, because he hath no son? Give unto us therefore a possession among the brethren of our father. And Moses brought their cause before the LORD." God told Moses that the daughters were right and should be given an inheritance among their family. Moreover, God said, "And thou shalt speak unto the children of Israel, saying, If a man die, and have no son, then ye shall cause his inheritance to pass unto his daughter." It appears that the laws were adjusted at the appeal of five concerned daughters.

Appeal. *How do I put it into practice?* I was still thinking about the advantages and methods of its use when I peeled apples for apple crisp. As my paring knife exposed the white flesh of the apple I captured a picture of appealing. (Yes, a peeling taught me about appealing.)

"The apple is red," a husband may say. The wife may declare that, of course, it is white. She can march over to him, grab the apple, and peel away most of the skin. She may even announce, "I told you so." But if a wife wishes to honor God and her husband, she can quietly appeal: "I know, dear, that the apple looks red. I would like you to see it from my perspective." Meekly she peels away some of the red skin to reveal the crisp, white flesh of the apple, while accepting the possibility that her husband may continue to call the apple red.

An appeal is made when your perspective differs from that of your husband or spiritual leader. He sees red. You see white. Of course the color of apples is not a significant issue to appeal! Apply the same basic principles to more serious matters. When your doubts, fears, intuition, perception, or conviction collides with your husband's perspective and decisions, you can make a graceful appeal. Appeal when you feel strongly about a matter, or when you sense danger or detriment to yourself or others. A graceful appeal includes allowing your husband or leader to make the final decision. That is still the essence of godly submission.

Take time to learn the art of appealing. Most husbands find it appealing. I suppose yours will too.

11. *Reading to Build*

On a hot, humid afternoon in July, I browsed under the tent beside our local library. Books loaded the tables and spilled into boxes that dotted the ground. The annual used book sale had attracted a number of shoppers. One young mother balanced a complaining baby on one hip while a toddler pulled on her skirt from the other side. I felt a sudden urge to rescue her from the clutches of the table over which she lingered, pulling out one paperback after another from the tightly stacked rows. "Romance Novels" read the label at the end of the table. Remembering the few minutes left for personal reading when I was at her stage of mothering, I wished to guide her to more profitable reading. How could her husband compete with the dashing, charming men pictured passionately on the front covers?

Marriages have been soured by wives who expect their husbands to emit the same sweetness of romance novel characters. Even a steady diet of "Christian romance" can tear down rather than build up. Blessed is the husband whose wife protects her mind from cheap reading and chooses rather to read books which build her character and their relationship.

 ## 12. Cultivating Feminine Friendships

"Do friendships with other women help you be a better wife?" I asked a close friend.

"Oh, yes," she answered with assurance.

"In what ways?"

"Well, a woman can often understand your emotions better than a man can." She paused. "Another woman tends to be a compassionate listener." Another pause, and then a chuckle. "It's like this: we think with our hearts; our husbands think with their heads."

Sometimes a woman wants to be *heard* from the heart, not just *fixed* from the head. There are times she wants to share tears with another woman because she knows she will be understood from the softness of a woman's heart. Not that she spurns her husband's strength or wisdom; not that he cannot learn to listen more compassionately. But a wife can receive from another woman what a husband finds difficult to give. The results? A mood-improved wife and a relieved husband. Close friendships with other women help a wife demand less of her husband.

A husband may feel threatened by his wife's close communication with friends. She may be guilty of husband-bashing. What husband relishes being the center of a women's criticism party? On the other hand, women can help each other understand their husbands and speak about them respectfully. How grateful I am for close women friends who have lightened the burdens of my heart, while calling me toward respectful responses to my husband and others.

"I will blow the chaff away," assures my friend with a pat on the back after I've vented frustrations about circumstances that trouble me. In so doing she helps me glean grain after the threshing. If you do not have such a woman friend, seek for one — and be one!

13. Respecting Respect

Review the brush strokes we have cited. Accept your honorable occupation. Be prudent. Allow your desires to be directed and adjust your expectations. Change as needed; give up twiddling or tightly gripping and strive to be a taut cord for your bow. Teach tenderly about love. Say no to nagging and appeal with grace. Read to build and cultivate feminine friendships. Behind each recommendation is a crucial, underlying principle — respect.

Daughters of God learn to value and respect respect. Note that Scriptures command husbands to love and wives to respect. By God's design, wives naturally love and respond to love. Husbands desire and respond to respect. Want your husband to love you more? Try respecting him more.

Love and respect are the primary brush strokes — the ones that outline and guide the rest of our painting of marriage. Without love and respect, detailed brush strokes of various colors clash and collide, painting a wrong message.

Our Biblical Example

Aquila and Priscilla painted a beautiful picture of togetherness in marriage. The Apostle Paul found them to be partners in business (Acts 18:3), in travel (Acts 18:18), and in Christian discipleship (Acts 18:24-26). Their effective working together for the Lord prompted Paul to greet them as "my helpers in Christ Jesus: who have for my life laid down their own necks" (Romans 16:3, 4). Together they ministered to the Gentile churches in such a way that all were thankful for them (Romans 16:4). What an effective bow and cord they were, propelling new believers into faithful service.

Most of us can improve our marital paintings by adjusting our brush strokes. Do not give up hope for a more beautiful painting, but do not demand it. Do your part as a daughter of God to paint with purpose. Learn to rest in God, wait on His timing, and leave the outcome to Him. If you are discouraged by dark splotches on your painting, remember that daisies often have dark centers. Brush bright splashes of petals around dark splotches by responding in prudent, respectful ways.

Delight in your bow and his bending for you. Bless him with tautness.

Enjoy the privilege of painting and the rich, precious gift of marriage!

Scriptures

"Marriage is honourable in all, and the bed undefiled:
but whoremongers and adulterers God will judge."
Hebrews 13:4

"Let the husband render unto
the wife due benevolence:
and likewise also the wife unto the husband."
1 Corinthians 7:3

"Let us be glad and rejoice, and give honour to him:
for the marriage of the Lamb is come,
and his wife hath made herself ready."
Revelation 19:7

Prayer

Dear God,

I commit myself and my husband to You. I commit our marriage and our dreams to You. Instill in us the seriousness of painting a picture of Your love for believers on the canvas of our marriage. Help me not to expect perfection but to look to the future in hope and improve my brush strokes as a wife.

Thank you for my bow. Untangle my twiddling or loosen my tight grip as necessary. Help me to twang in ready submission and tautly bend my bow per Your directions.

Direct our painting with the primary brush strokes of love and respect.

And Father, thank You for trusting Your daughter with this honorable occupation, this precious gift.

Painting With Purpose,

CHAPTER 10

Serving Alone

*W*omen who serve God without the spiritual direction of a husband face a unique set of problems. Scenarios vary: The widow serves God alone. So does the woman whose husband has deserted her. The wife of an unbelieving husband serves God alone, as does the wife who has been divorced against her will. To a lesser degree, the wife of a backslidden or spiritually stagnated man serves God in a lonely way. Trying to determine whose grief is greater is pointless; all who serve alone experience periods of intense loneliness and agony of soul. Their pain is not beyond the reach of our merciful and compassionate God. His arms sustain them in a gentle way when they turn tearstained faces toward His.

Remembering my own mother's tears and frustrations, I sometimes feel now the burden that I did then. I wish I could "fix" what is broken. In that very typical daughter-of-Eve-like response, I wish I could list here methods guaranteed to produce desirable results. Something like: "Take these four easy steps to secure the spiritual leadership you desire." Although you and

151

I cannot breathe spiritual life into resistant husbands, nor ease a widow's grief, we do serve a God who can.

"Is God hiding His face? Will our prayers be answered? Do others care?" I have asked myself these heart-wrenching questions while reaching out to women who serve alone. While I wrestled with what to write to encourage daughters of God along a lonely path, God introduced me to DeeDee.

We Can Pray

"When will Chapter 10 be finished?" DeeDee's dark eyes pierced my soul. I had given her Chapter 9 to review, hoping to encourage her in a faithful response to her yet unconverted husband. "I really need Chapter 10. I don't know how much longer I can hold on. You mentioned in Chapter 9 that we would meet some women who . . ." Her voice trailed off and I nodded, remembering the promise I had written.

"Women who serve God alone?"

"Yes! What do they have to say? What does the Bible say? Sometimes I think my husband is this close to being saved." She held her thumb and forefinger about an inch apart. "But I don't know — Vern's skeptical." One look into her expectant face convinced me that she earnestly wanted her husband to know the joy of salvation that she had so recently experienced.

"The Bible offers hope," I said. But I winced, knowing I could not promise that her husband would become a believer. "But God will not force your husband to serve Him. Each of us must make a personal choice."

"Yes, I understand that."

"The devil does not want your husband to be adopted into God's family," I said as I thought of husbands held tightly in the deceiver's grasp.

"I know he doesn't." DeeDee nodded and added, "The devil doesn't even play fair when he tempts us to serve him. We don't have to worship him, just love someone or something else more than we love God."

I agreed. *How much she has learned already in the short time since her salvation,* I marveled.

"We can pray," I began and thought of the women I knew who prayed for years for their husband's salvation.

"Oh, I am, I am." Her head nodded vigorously.

"God's timing is not always according to our desires," I cautioned as I thought of my own mother's nearly fifty years of prayer. I recalled how they were answered less than two years before debilitating strokes robbed my father of much of his newfound joy in Christ. "But there are women who testify of God's faithfulness," I hurried to add. "Let's read what the Bible has to say." We paged to 1 Corinthians 7:13, 14, 16 and read the Scripture together:

"And the woman which hath an husband that believeth not, and if he be pleased to dwell with her, let her not leave him. For the unbelieving husband is sanctified by the wife, and the unbelieving wife is sanctified by the husband: For what knowest thou, O wife, whether thou shalt save thy husband? Or how knowest thou, O man, whether thou shalt save thy wife?"

I told DeeDee I did not understand all the Scripture we read but that "sanctify" means to set apart for God or to grow in holiness. Vern's likelihood of accepting the Lord was much greater because *she* believed. With God's help she could show a picture of Christ's holiness and draw her husband toward God.

We studied some other Scriptures and prayed aloud together before ending our Bible study for the evening. I rejoiced in her hope and prayed that God would answer her prayers according to His will.

At home my pencil dragged heavily. My mind circled in perplexity. Did I have anything hopeful to offer women who served God alone? I searched my memory for women whose husbands did become believers. My list was dishearteningly small. Most of the women I had known who had unbelieving or backslidden husbands had learned to live life alone or adjusted to their husbands' resistance toward spiritual things. A few of them had a reasonable hope that God's saving grace had pardoned their loved ones' souls in the final hours of life. Others prayed on.

Reviewing the list again, I thought of the character traits displayed in these women: Persistence in prayer. Patience. Compassion for others. Desire to follow God. Love of the Word. Their adoration for God beamed brightly from their dark circumstances. Their dependence on Him evidenced true faith. I had to agree with our pastor who said, "God gives a special grace to women whose husbands are unbelievers. He cares for them in an extraordinary way."

And what of widows within our midst? Years of serving God together have been shortened and now they also serve God alone. The Bible quite often refers to the care of widows, so women who serve God alone must be close to His heart — physical widows and spiritual widows.

I picked up the Word and my pencil and determined to quiet my circling, doubting thoughts with truth.

"There hath no temptation taken you but such as is common to man: but God is faithful, who will not suffer you to be tempted above that ye are able; but will with the temptation also make a way to escape, that ye may be able to bear it." God's promise in 1 Corinthians 10:13 offers hope. No matter how much a widow, a

154

deserted wife, or a wife who believes alone feels that her circumstances are unbearable, she can have the assurance that God's grace can lift the heavy load.

Load-Lifting

The enemy of our souls tries to load us with burdens that seem too heavy to lift. In Deuteronomy 33:27 we find words that are especially load-lifting: "The eternal God is thy refuge, and underneath are the everlasting arms: and he shall thrust out the enemy from before thee." Possibly the devil considers widows and wives who serve God alone easy prey, for it would seem that their adverse circumstances are to his advantage.

He tells the widow it is not fair. He makes her loneliness seem black and bottomless. He tempts her to languish away hours that could be used for God's glory.

He tells the wife of an unbeliever that her husband is beyond hope. As years pass, he slyly whispers that she is responsible: "After all, if you would live a good-enough life, he might turn to God." Carefully the devil mixes a sludge of guilt and discouragement and pushes the wife toward it.

For the wife who has been deserted, the devil heaps smothering feathers of self-pity mixed with seeds of doubt and nettles of rejection. Then he tries to convince her to jump into the softness. How true it is — he does not fight fair!

Enter God. The eternal God. The God whose everlasting arms are longer and stronger than any weapon of the enemy. Oh, what peace and rest for the tempted! When life is not fair, when the pain sears, when the load is heavy, the eternal God is thy refuge. *He* can fill the emptiness. *He* can lift the load. *He* is everything the hurting heart desires.

An Answer

Armed with other Scriptures of hope and comfort, I met again with DeeDee for Bible study. "Do you have a testimony of what God is doing for you?" I asked, eager for a word of encouragement after a particularly trying day.

"I do, I do!" DeeDee beamed. Her hand trembled with excitement as she reached to touch mine. "He did it! He prayed the prayer—Vern accepted Christ as his personal Saviour!"

I am ashamed to confess that my mouth dropped open in surprise. *O ye of little faith,* I chided myself with the Lord's words. My gaping mouth turned into a wide smile as I listened to DeeDee's account of her husband's salvation. We praised the Lord for His goodness; then we hopscotched through His Word like two delighted schoolgirls at recess.

"Remember you showed me 1 Corinthians 7?" DeeDee asked. "Well, I prayed often that God would sanctify my husband through me. Vern saw the change in me since I accepted Christ and it made him wish he could have faith like I did. At first I wanted to pressure him to accept Christ, but I remembered 2 Timothy 2:24: 'The servant of the Lord must not strive; but be gentle unto all men, apt to teach, patient.' I remembered that a prudent wife is patient, and I tried very hard to be prudent." (Again I marveled at how quickly this babe in Christ assimilated Biblical truths.) "Oh, yes," she continued, "I have been reading in Luke 18 about the unjust judge. I did just as it says here," DeeDee pointed to verses one to eight. "I continued knocking."

At home that evening my thoughts outran my pen. God's grace had enabled DeeDee to have a sanctifying effect on her husband. She had persisted in prayer. God had answered in a marvelous way; less than three months had passed since we had begun praying fervently for her husband. I was challenged by her faith and chastened for my own doubting and fears. "I still need Chapter 10," DeeDee said when we parted. I hurried to the computer. Little did she know how much she was helping me write this chapter that had stalled with uncertainty.

Other Answers

Not every lonely wife's prayers are answered in the way DeeDee's were. Nor do I suggest that one's faith is insufficient if persistent prayer is not rewarded in the way a wife desires or when she desires. God is not a one-answer God. Sometimes His answer to heartfelt prayers is "No" or "Wait." He gives a special grace to those who pray for years without receiving answers. Always we can glorify His name through the answers He gives—or the ones He does not give.

Grace, evident in the life of a suffering Christian, is a powerful witness of faith. I have observed grace applied abundantly to women who continue knocking on God's door with sincere prayers for the souls of loved ones.

Do you know mothers who continue to pray fervently for daughters and sons who are bent on following in the wayward footsteps of backslidden or unbelieving fathers? "The devil just wants me to give up praying," says one. "I guess all I can do is to pray and fast even more." While this mother grieves for her husband and son, she sees them taking steps toward God, and we see her growing in faith and commitment to God and prayer. God's name is being glorified by her faithfulness.

Mary's husband softened in the last seven years of his life. He returned to her home after having deserted her and the children many years before. He showed much interest in spiritual things, but on the day of his death his life was still marked by indecision. Even in the face of uncertainty, Mary continued to praise God for all the prayers He had answered. "Why, one time God woke me out of a deep sleep and suggested a place to look for the check I had lost." Her aging eyes widened and her wrinkles rearranged above arched eyebrows as she told me the story. "That check was important. I did not want to lose that amount of money. I got right up and looked. Sure enough, I found it at the bottom of a bag of trash—and just a few hours before it would have been destroyed!"

No one doubted Mary's faith. Even after her death, her testimonies, when remembered, encouraged others to walk in faith. Mary accepted the answers she received. She did not fret about the prayers that were not answered according to her desires. Her life of faith glorified God.

Several years ago, during weeks of illness, I struggled while my faith shuddered. One day I received a get-well card from my aunt. It was full of encouraging words and Scriptures. "Cast thy burden upon the LORD, and he shall sustain thee: he shall never suffer the righteous to be moved" (Psalm 55:22) was printed in the upper corner of the card, followed by these words and initials: "Tested, tried, and true! —MKB."

I recalled the events that must have made this verse

a favorite: My uncle had moved away from home, never to return, when the youngest of their seven living children was an infant. Aunt K. clung to the Lord as she stayed in the home, sewing and babysitting to add to the older children's earnings and thus support the family. I visited their home often and have pleasant memories of days spent there. But a few tense-filled days surface in my memory with whisperings about their home possibly being sold. Even my young mind reeled at the impact that would have on the family of my favorite cousins. The move never materialized, and we children returned to building our stick houses in the woods that bordered the property. We didn't have to give up our carefully designed play homes, and my aunt did not have to part with hers. Fear etched our minds at times, and sadness tugged at our hearts, but we rested in the God of our mothers. I knew the initialed verse on my get-well card really had been tested, tried, and true for Aunt K. Her testimony of faith bolstered my own staggering faith.

My mother's faithfulness and obedience to God and her persistence in prayer brought glory to God even while she waited and prayed all those years. Once a doctor commented on her calloused knees; years of scrubbing floors and praying at her bedside had left their mark. I remember her spontaneous, on-her-feet prayers, prayed aloud as if she were talking to a friend or a spouse. She prayed over lawn mowers that would not start, cars that produced a variety of anxiety-producing sounds, a flooded basement, and snow-drifted roads. I remember her "borrowing" tithe money on occasion with a prayer and a promise. "Make ends meet Lord; I will repay You." Often she prayed that God would provide godly husbands for her daughters. Whatever the challenge, she tackled it to the best of her ability, with a heart full of prayer.

Mother's prayers were not always pleas for help. "Oh, thank You, Lord; we made it!" Praise erupted naturally. She learned from a dear elderly friend to add postscripts to her prayers. Sometimes at our kitchen table or elsewhere, Mother would close her eyes again, and add to a prayer, "And as Dr. Elizabeth would say, 'P.S., Lord . . .' " Then she would bring to the Lord the matter she had forgotten to mention before the amen.

In persistent entreaty, spontaneous praise, and personal postscripts, Mother mentored me in prayer. I knew God did not answer all our prayers according to our wishes, but I saw His grace sustain and bless us.

As I write this our nation is clamoring about Hollywood's latest interpretation of Christ's Crucifixion; I have no desire to see the graphic portrayal. Last week I sat several pews behind my mother as our congregation took part in the Communion service, commemorating Christ's death. Several times I saw my mother wipe tears from her eyes. I was filled with a warm rush of love and memories. I sent the Lord a quick P.S. I thanked Him for the lessons about the suffering of Christ as Mother's tears dropped on my head that lay nestled in her lap during long-ago Communion services. I never doubted that she knew and loved the Lord intimately, and that she identified deeply with His suffering.

Although our circumstances were less comfortable than those of many families I knew, our little home was rich in soil for spiritual growth. Over the years God redeemed our suffering, exchanging it for grace and applying value to the unanswered prayers. The glory belongs to God.

If you serve God alone, know that He hears your prayers. Trust Him to answer according to His wisdom. Give your husband and your grief to God again and again. Refuse to allow your relationship with God to be ruined by a husband's death or his unrighteous decisions. Daughters of God have the wonderful privilege of accepting loneliness as God's invitation to receive of His grace, rise above the circumstances, and seek Him face-to-face.

The poem that follows was written by a widow who lost her life partner. Together they had served for many years in a Christian publishing ministry. Only four months after her husband's casket closed, she lost her adult son to death as well. The booklet of poems she published in memory of her husband and son holds rich truths of God's grace.

Grace Enough

Every trial passes through
God's loving outstretched hands,
And none too hard will ever come
Because He understands.
He knows the places we are weak;
He knows where we are strong;
He knows how much we need His aid
And sends His strength along.
So by His grace we can endure,
Not failing any test;
For when our weakest moments come,
God's strength is at its best.[1]

—Merna B. Shank

Abigail's Attitude and Answer

Abigail, wife of Nabal, received a remarkable answer to the cries of her heart. Her surly husband paid for his obstinate behavior with his life, and eventually she became a king's wife instead (see 1 Samuel 25).

After a close encounter with jealous King Saul, David and his men continued to hide in the wilderness. In sore need of provisions, David sent men to wealthy Nabal to ask for donations in return for the protection his men had provided Nabal's shepherds. Nabal rudely turned them away empty-handed. David and his men set off to repay Nabal's selfishness with the sword, but Abigail learned of her husband's evil doings and hastened to act.

Abigail's attitude and actions provide guidance for women whose husbands plunge them into perplexing or dangerous situations. First, she listened to the warnings of another regarding their predicament (verse 17). Second, she took action, preparing food to appease the anger of David and his men. By her actions she sought to save her own life and the life of her husband and household. Third, she did not disclose her plans to her husband. (In general it is unwise for a wife to be sneaky in dealing with her husband, but if the husband is "such a son of Belial, that a man cannot speak to him" [verse 17], then a wife is not likely to reason with him either. Women in Abigail's shoes may need to act at times without asking permission, but *only* when it is wise to do so.)

When Abigail greeted David she humbled herself (verses 23, 24). Humbling oneself in an already embarrassing situation is difficult to do. Wives who step out in courage and humbly ask for help are to be commended. Abigail did not lie about her husband and his folly (verse 25). She honestly addressed it. Note, however, that she showed respect toward him by not being critical in his presence. Abigail pleaded for her life and the life of her husband by appealing to David's integrity (verses 26 and 31). Last, Abigail expressed her need. "When the LORD shall have dealt well with [thee], then remember thine handmaid" (verse 31).

When the raisins, cakes, and figs had been devoured and Nabal's drunken stupor had abated, Abigail told him the truth about what she had done. Nabal's "heart died within him, and he became as a stone"(verse 37). Ten days later he died. David not only remembered Abigail, he also asked to marry her. Any woman who has lived in fear of abusive anger will quickly note that God handled Nabal; Abigail did not have to.

David said to Abigail, "Blessed be thy advice, and blessed be thou" (verse 33). We may also gather advice from Abigail's actions. If your husband is like Nabal,

1. Heed good advice.

2. Take action for the sake of yourself, your husband, and your children.

3. Be wise and discerning in communication.

4. Humble yourself. Ask for help.

5. Honestly address your husband's faults but . . .

6. Be careful to respect him.

7. Plead with those in authority on behalf of yourself and your husband.

8. Express the needs of your heart when appropriate.

9. Be honest with your husband. After anger abates, one may say, "I care enough about you and our marriage that I have asked for help."

Carefully balance Abigail's actions with New Testament principles. Ask God to help you be discerning and prudent. Obey your husband to the best of your ability, remembering Peter's advice in Acts 5:29: "We ought to obey God rather than men." If you are being battered, seek help. God can give grace, protection, and a means of escape.

Consider also Eunice and Lois (2 Timothy 1:5). Although Timothy's father was apparently an unbeliever, his grandmother and mother acted wisely by teaching him about genuine faith in God. Faithful action on the part of prudent women goes a long way in teaching the next generation about God.

Teaching Alone of God's Ways

Women who serve God alone face a great — but not impossible — challenge in passing faith on to their children. Children of broken homes or children who have lost a parent to death face questions and struggles unique to their situation. Anger about their circumstances may grow into bitterness and rebellion. The lifestyle of an unbelieving or backslidden parent may look attractive to a hurting child. Boundaries and guidelines of the believing parent may be seen as confining and unnecessary. Sometimes a child who has willingly followed the path of the believing parent may suddenly take bold steps toward what they know to be wrong when they reach adolescence or young adulthood. What does a widow or a deserted wife do when she faces these challenges?

Pray. Prayer is paramount. Pray for, and with, your children. When you do not know how to pray for their needs, simply repeat each hurting child's name again and again before the throne, releasing each one to

God's faithful care. God does not expect you to raise your children alone. He has promised to be a Father of the fatherless and a Judge of the widows. "Let us therefore come boldly unto the throne of grace, that we may obtain mercy, and find grace to help in time of need" (Hebrews 4:16).

Obey. If you want your children to obey, model obedience to your authorities. Obedience to an unbelieving husband is especially difficult if he asks you to do things contrary to God's commands. Those who have experienced this situation understand the predicament you face. On one hand, you want to obey God's commands. On the other hand, if you stay true to your convictions, you may end up disobeying God's command to submit to your husband. Obey when you are able to obey without violating Biblical commands. And remember, respectful appeals to a husband go a long way in obtaining his favor and permission to live by your convictions.

Stay. *Stay stable* in your beliefs. Your children may push for change, but stability is often what they crave. *Stay committed* to your spouse as much as possible. Remember that cutting remarks and frequent criticism of your child's other parent leave lasting scars. *Stay connected* with your children. Talk openly and honestly with them. Reach for their hearts and do not brush aside their suffering. Be honest about your own feelings and let them see your faith. *Stay true* to God even when the path you walk narrows with loneliness, and treacherously descends into valleys of despair. Your path will climb again. New heights await the faithful daughter of God.

Climbing the Ladder of Respect

"How can I show respect to my husband when he

doesn't show love to me?" asks a distraught wife.

She may learn to climb a ladder of respect. According to the dictionary, *deference*, *respect*, and *regard* are synonyms. We give *deference* to one we consider superior in position or attainment. We show *respect* to those who are felt to be worthy. *Regard* is felt for those who are admirable. In other words, our attitude makes the difference. Starting on the bottom rung, a wife can strive to give deference to her husband because of his position. With effort she can climb to the rung of respect.

Husbands frequently respond favorably to respect (they desire it just as wives desire love), so a wife may be able to move up another rung to regard her man. Reverence is the Biblical recommendation for a wife's relationship to her husband (Ephesians 5:33). That sounds like a top rung, does it not? Climbing is hard work. Sometimes we slip or fall, but that does not mean we should quit reaching for the top rung.

Women who have been deserted or are married to Nabal-like men benefit from climbing a ladder of self-respect as well. A sense of shame may weigh down their feet, and the stigma they so easily feel may stumble the steps they try to climb above the reproach.

Focusing on God's mercy, acceptance, and grace refreshes weary feet. "I have often found comfort in Isaiah 54, especially verses four to eight," said one woman as she spoke tearfully of the rejection and reproach she experienced, having been divorced against her will. Christians holding a position against divorce tended to distance themselves from her, shielding themselves from her pain. "For all these years, God has been my Husband," she said. "He is my Rock." What a testimony of God's faithfulness!

Learning Repose

For forty-two years she worked by his side. He never lost his zeal for missions, which first grabbed his heart in high school. Time and time again he answered God's call: to the ministry, to evangelism, to start a Christian school, to a time of service on the mission field, and to ministries for those in need. Lester saw the visions, and Betty stood beside him, supporting him through the realization of each one. At the heart of it all was their passionate desire to share the love of Jesus.

While Lester and Betty ministered in one community after another, a virus attacked the blood vessels of Lester's body, causing tumors to grow, affecting his health in such a way that seven surgeries were required. Each time his body suffered, his spirit grew stronger. Time spent convalescing was filled with learning more about God and how to minister to others. Then the virus made one last, vicious attack.

Betty stood faithfully by her husband's bedside, joined when possible by their children. Carefully she recorded all the details of a service he wished to hold on December 30, "to praise God for my healing." For days he talked vividly of Heaven. ("Don't you see the mansions? Oh, tell everyone they are so much more beautiful than I said they would be!") Then Lester left Betty's side and passed on to the streets of Glory. The service on December 30 became his funeral.

"Jesus was right there beside me," Betty relates. "He became my Husband. I leaned on Jesus before, but now I depend on Him in a new way. I really feel blessed by the support of family, friends, and the church. Before Lester died, he told me, 'I want you to tell everyone to be faithful. Keep on in your work with women. Encourage them in the faith.' So God sends me forth with the blessing of my husband and my children. I am too blessed to be depressed. I cry. I miss Lester. But God has energized me to continue reaching out to share the love of Jesus. His presence is empowering — and that is grace."

First it was the car that needed to be replaced, then the refrigerator and the washing machine. The latest appliance to quit was her freezer full of food, but Betty finds many reasons to praise God. In the three years since Lester's death, Betty has faced attacks of the enemy, but her resolve is clear, her faith is undaunted, and her repose in the Lord is sweet.

Our Heavenly Father

When burdens weigh you down with care
And heartaches threaten to despair,
There is an avenue of prayer
    That reaches God the Father.

When struggles make you weep and sigh
And tempt your mind to question why,
There's One who's touched with every cry —
    A gentle heavenly Father.

Our Father every struggle knows.
He tempers every wind that blows
And grants His children sweet repose —
    Our loving heavenly Father.[2]
                 — Merna B. Shank

Take heart, Daughter of God. Repose really is possible when you rest in the arms of God.

From Mount Pisgah's Lofty Height

Servants of the Lord may find themselves on Mount Pisgah's lofty height.

"And Moses went up from the plains of Moab unto the mountain . . . to the top of Pisgah. And the LORD shewed him all the land . . . And the LORD said unto him, This is the land which I sware unto Abraham, unto Isaac, and unto Jacob, saying, I will give it unto thy seed: I have caused thee to see it with thine eyes, but thou shalt not go over thither" (Deuteronomy 34: 1, 4).

Wait a minute, God, is that fair? After all the children of Israel put Moses through? After all he did for them? And You called him to do it. God, what did You have in mind? Our humanness begs us to ask the questions.

"So Moses the servant of the LORD died there in the land of Moab, according to the word of the LORD. And he buried him in a valley in the land of Moab . . . but no man knoweth of his sepulchre unto this day" (verses 5, 6).

Fairness is not the issue. God is sovereign. Though He withheld the blessing of living in the promised land from His servant, He buried Moses. A private crossing to eternity. A private funeral. With God officiating and laying His servant to rest.

"And there arose not a prophet since in Israel like unto Moses, whom the LORD knew face to face" (verse 10).

Imagine what it is like to be known of God *face-to-face.* From the depths of Deuteronomy comes a message of hope. Women may be called to serve God wholeheartedly as Moses was. But God may choose to allow them to serve Him alone. Fairness is not the issue. God is sovereign. He wants to bless some people with what they *do not have* or what they *do not receive.* God wants to see their faces turn to Him. He wants to know them face-to- face. Women who serve God alone are precious daughters in His sight.

> "Face to face with Christ, my Saviour,
> face to face — what will it be?
> When with rapture I behold Him,
> Jesus Christ who died for me!
>
> Only faintly now I see Him,
> with the darkling veil between;
> But a blessed day is coming,
> when His glory shall be seen.
>
> What rejoicing in His presence,
> when are banished grief and pain,
> When the crooked ways are straightened,
> and the dark things shall be plain.
>
> Face to face! Oh, blissful moment!
> Face to face — to see and know;
> Face to face with my Redeemer,
> Jesus Christ who loves me so.
>
> **Chorus:**
> Face to face shall I behold Him,
> Far beyond the starry sky;
> Face to face, in all His glory,
> I shall see Him by and by![3]

The words of this hymn, so beautifully penned by a busy wife and mother, Carrie E. Breck, speak of the wonder we know now, and the rapture we will behold. Of her writing Carrie said, "I penciled verses under all conditions; over a mending basket, with a baby on my arm, and sometimes even when sweeping or washing dishes, my mind moved in poetic meter."[4]

From Moses of old and yesterday's busy daughter of God, we are encouraged to seek Christ face-to-face. No woman who serves God alone should overlook the privilege.

Hiccups to Heaven

Prayers may be answered in miraculous ways. In our family the hiccups brought about redemption. For four days my father hiccupped nonstop. Nothing he tried relieved his misery. Weak from lack of sleep and the continual heaving of his diaphragm, Daddy allowed Mother to take him to the hospital. When I visited him the next day he seemed more than just physically relieved. His chest no longer jumped and his eyes held glimmers of peace. He thanked me when I prayed for him. "You'll never know how much I prayed the past four days," he said.

I hesitated a moment, sensing a peace in that hospital room that I wanted to grab and confirm before I clasped it to my longing heart. *The last time I asked him about his soul he got so angry that I promised never to ask again. Dare I try once more?*

"Your soul, Daddy . . . ?" I left the question dangle unfinished, hoping, praying, that the peace I felt would not be shot full of holes.

He turned to face me. Without flinching, his eyes met mine and he said calmly, "It is okay."

Hiccups over, my father settled back in his easy chair and life went on much as it had before. That chair was still more comfortable than a church pew; angry comments about religion and the people who had tried to convert him still erupted. But we noticed a softening of his ways.

I confess that my prayers wore thin and I wondered if Daddy would ever lay down his burden of bitterness, but God was still at work. Several years later my father was rushed to the hospital with full-blown congestive heart failure. Our family gathered outside the Intensive Care Unit while Daddy struggled to breathe. "He could hardly answer me between labored breaths," reported our pastor, "but it is well with his soul."

We breathed easier, but during the night Daddy's condition worsened. For two days he wavered between life and death. When the worst of the ordeal was over, and he was moved out of Intensive Care, Daddy's roommate handed him a Gospel tract. At the bottom of the tract was a place to sign one's name if he prayed and accepted salvation. How thrilled we were to see Dad's familiar signature. Mother and Daddy hung that signed tract on the wall of their home and change ensued. The easy chair was vacant on Sunday mornings and most Sunday evenings as my parents went to Mother's church, to Daddy's church, and to the church down the road. Never again did I hear the name of a pastor, whom he'd hated bitterly, seethe through my father's clenched jaw. He really had changed. Whom could we praise but God?

Pray on, dear sister, as you serve God alone. Be strengthened in God's grace. Cling to your Rock of Refuge.

To you who surround her, do not turn from her suffering. Pray for and with her. Support her in ways you can. Be role models for her children and listen patiently when they need to vent their frustrations. Walk a path of peace and joy before them, praying they will follow.

Dare to slay the slander and push stigmas aside. Learn to weep with the widow. Look into the face of a daughter — who intimately knows the Father.

Before this manuscript reached the printer, my friend DeeDee lost her beloved husband, Vern, to a tragic automobile accident. A few short years ago their experiences with prayer and salvation helped me write this chapter. Now DeeDee weeps with other widows, and I cry with her. But not all our tears are tears of grief. We have shed tears of *joy* for the *hope* and *peace* God promises in the Scriptures, including the ones that follow.

Scriptures

"The LORD also will be a refuge for the oppressed,
a refuge in times of trouble.
And they that know thy name
will put their trust in thee:
for thou, LORD, hast not forsaken them that seek thee."
Psalm 9:9, 10

"But let the righteous be glad;
let them rejoice before God:
yea, let them exceedingly rejoice.
Sing unto God . . . and rejoice before him.
A father of the fatherless, and a judge of
the widows, is God in his holy habitation.
God setteth the solitary in families."
Psalm 68:3-6

"Fear not; for thou shalt not be ashamed:
neither be thou confounded;
for thou shalt not be put to shame:
for thou shalt forget the shame of thy youth,
and shalt not remember the reproach
of thy widowhood any more.
For thy Maker is thine husband;
the LORD of hosts is his name;
and thy Redeemer the Holy One of Israel;
The God of the whole earth shall he be called.
For the LORD hath called thee as a woman
forsaken and grieved in spirit,
and a wife of youth,
when thou wast refused, saith thy God . . . .
But with great mercies will I gather thee."
Isaiah 54:4-6, 7

Prayer

Dear Father,
   *Help me to be faithful in reaching out to women who serve
You alone.*

                Sincerely,

_____

(Prayer written by Aunt K.)

Dear Father,

Thank You that You are God. You are sovereign, the Great "I Am," and yet You are mindful of me as Your daughter. Thank You that You are always there, even in the lonely night hours. You never sleep nor slumber (Psalm 121:4). Your name, Lord, "is a strong tower: the righteous runneth into it, and is safe" (Proverbs 18:10). No matter how great or minor my struggles, You love me. You care and understand. Thank You for the comfort I have received from You. Help me to take that comfort and extend it to others who are serving alone. Thank You for the joy of the Lord, which is my strength (Nehemiah 8:10). Fill my heart with Your love and compassion; give me a listening ear and words of encouragement to those serving alone, as well as to others.

Thank You, Jesus!

(Even in the last hours of life as she struggled with cancer, Aunt K. was a blessing to others including other women who serve God alone. Seven children tenderly, faithfully cared for their mother who had faithfully cared for them. Aunt K. passed away before she saw this prayer in print.)

EXTENDING
GRACE
TO OTHERS

CHAPTER 11

Passing the Faith Along

$\mathcal{M}$y teenager was in tears. Someone for whom she had provided many hours of free service had dragged her name through the dirt and shoved a tarnished reputation into the face of one of her closest friends. "It isn't right! After all I've done for her, and then she talks like that about me." Hot tears spilled on my shoulder as I gave my daughter a comforting hug. My heart ached, partly because of her pain, and partly because I feared that my own failures had put her reputation at risk. I knew God had forgiven me, but the consequences were not easily wiped away. *How can I offer her hope?* My mind traveled back over similar circumstances, times when I had been rewarded evil for good. I remembered drawing strength from one Scripture especially. "Read 1 Peter 2:19-21 before you go to sleep tonight," I encouraged my daughter when I said good night.

What would I do without a faith to pass along? I wondered. *How could I go to sleep in peace if I did not trust my Sovereign Lord to care for and comfort my daughter?* How could any parent encourage children to stand strong without a faith to sustain them when their world is crumbling?

Throughout our busy days as daughters of Eve, caring for the many things women are called to care for, we can live as daughters of God and pass the faith along to the next generations.

Faith. It is the shield "wherewith ye shall be able to quench all the fiery darts of the wicked" (Ephesians 6:16). How sad if we were to help our children don the armor of God and forget to hand them the shield of faith. What if their reach for victory was shortened by an unshielded arm? Granted, faith has to be accepted and used by the child, but it is our responsibility as parents to offer it and praise its efficacy. "I know you have your armor, Child, but here is your shield. It will protect you in extraordinary ways. It protects the parts of you that are exposed. And it *quenches* those fiery darts of the devil so they do not start a fire at your feet. When the battle is fierce, My Child, crouch behind your faith."

Winsome Faith

Do my children see me enjoying God's Word? Do they hear me singing songs of praise and petition? Do they see evidences of my faith? When I am tested, does my family know I will lean heavily on the God who saved me? Do they look forward to gathering in the living room for family devotions?

I stepped into our bedroom, eager to exchange my new Sunday shoes for something more comfortable. A table full of wedding leftovers and boxes of items waited to be put away. It was hard to realize our oldest child was married now, and our family would never be the same. I felt relieved but weary, happy but sad. A beautiful Mother's Day card and two letters lay on our bed. I let the tears wash my smile as I read them — one from our daughter and one from her new husband. Each of them expressed their thanks and appreciation for many things. "Thank you for being the kind of people we can look to as an example," LaNell wrote. "I learned a lot about living a life that pleases God by watching you; and ever since I was very small, you've been teaching me."

Our new son-in-law wrote: "I am so happy to receive a wife who has been taught how to love God and her neighbors. I believe that so much of what makes LaNell the wonderful person she is, is because of your positive influence in her life." Need I say that more than my feet felt comforted as I left our bedroom to tackle the work that waited? What *incredible joy* to pass faith along!

Mothers and fathers know little eyes are often watching and little ears hear so much. What a challenge to display our faith attractively and worship before them! If we want teenage eyes and ears to turn toward the things of God, we need to be persistent and consistent in turning to Him ourselves.

Singles also are valuable faith passers. In my youth, my favorite Sunday school teacher was a single woman who displayed a winsome faith. I could see that faith had carried her through hard times. Her ready smile and the way she talked about the Lord appealed to my desire to trust the Lord. In later years we became close friends, even though a decade separated our ages. Never underestimate the potential you have as a single person to affect the lives of young people and pass the faith along.

"But if from thence thou shalt seek the LORD thy God,

thou shalt find him, if thou seek him with all thy heart and with all thy soul" (Deuteronomy 4:29). "Thou shalt keep therefore his statutes, and his commandments, which I command thee this day, that it may go well with thee, *and with thy children after thee*" (Deuteronomy 4:40, emphasis mine).

Seeking God with all the heart and soul displays a winsome faith.

Careful Faith

I stopped writing momentarily to take another load of laundry from my washing machine. Almost without thinking about it, I fastened dresses and shirts on hangers in the direction that would be most convenient for each family member when he or she reaches to take them from the closet. My husband's clothes hang on the left side of the closet, so his shirt buttons should face the right. My son's closet door opens to the right so his shirts hang facing left. Two daughters share closets, so the zippers of their dresses face left and right at opposite ends of the closet. I do not remember when I first became aware that I paid attention to such trifling details for my family members. It is a simple way to make their lives a bit easier. I do not rigidly adhere to the practice, and I suspect that my family members are totally unaware of my efforts. "Don't waste time over such little details," they might say. But by now, I am so used to the practice that it takes little effort to simplify their lives in this small way. (If you are wondering, I do not run a meticulous house with precision in every detail.)

As I hung the dresses and shirts on the back porch, I considered whether I attend to the spiritual needs of my family with the same emphasis on detail. When the children arrive home from school today will I listen carefully to accounts of their day? Will I see their troubles as invitations to encourage and model faith? Do I carefully find Scriptures to give backbone to our beliefs and answers to their questions? Am I careful in upholding Scriptural principles?

"And when thy son asketh thee in time to come, saying, What mean the testimonies, and the statutes, and the judgments, which the LORD our God hath commanded you? Then thou shalt say unto thy son, We were . . . bondmen . . . and the LORD brought us out . . . with a mighty hand." (Deuteronomy 6:20, 21).

Careful faith gives answers—answers based on Scripture and validated by personal testimony.

Challenged Faith

Faith is most profoundly visible when it is under trial. How do I respond when my faith is challenged? Am I willing to submit to God's refining fires?

At times I have buckled under trial. I gave way to panicky fears. My faith waned precariously thin. In the middle of the night I have tearfully asked the bedroom ceiling, "How can I pass faith along to my children when I don't have any to spare?"

Lately, dark forebodings such as these were brightened by a most precious thing—my children's faith. "I'm praying for you, Mom," my teenage daughter promised me with a warm hug. Recently I had helped to dry her tears; now she was touched by mine. My adult daughter listened compassionately while I unloaded my fears. She did not mock or sweep them away as insignificant. Her wise words were refreshing and Scriptural. "What can I do for you, Mom?" my adolescent son asked. I knew he had noticed the droop in my shoulders and the drag in my steps. His quiet way of coming alongside and encouraging me was so much like my husband's. I smiled through my fears.

Gradually my faith increased, especially after I poured out my heart in desperation and repentance. Circumstances had not changed. The fears still challenged my faith, but they had also strengthened my faith. I wondered whether trusting God only in the good times would really be faith?

Fire flames at faith from all angles. The devil aims his flaming arrows in a myriad of ways. Unbelievers hurl accusations or try to reduce to ashes the very foundations of our faith. Even other Christians can ignite fires that threaten to singe or smolder away at our faith.

In Hebrews 11, the hall of faith, faithful followers of God are commended for their faith. "Who through faith subdued kingdoms, wrought righteousness, obtained promises, stopped the mouths of lions, quenched the violence of fire . . . out of weakness were made strong, waxed valiant in fight." (Hebrews 11:33, 34).

It was faith that held our Anabaptist ancestors true to God while they burned at the stake; it is faith that will hold me when I face refining fires. What an effective tool for building faith in generations to come.

Chased Faith

Daughters of God know that sometimes the duties of life chase away a focus on faith. Monica Miller's poem expresses so well the battle in our hearts.

Mary's Heart

It's a Martha's world, dear Father,
With Martha's work to do
But give me Mary's heart, Lord,
That longs to sit with You.

To sit in silence, listening
With strengthened mind and will
For tallest cares grow smaller
Sometimes by keeping still.
   By keeping still within, Lord,
   And gathering from Your strength
   For Mary's soul grows faint, as
   Does Martha's heart at length.
      Help me to do with patience
      What Martha's hands must do
      But give me Mary's heart, Lord,
      That draws its strength from You.

— Monica Miller (Used by permission.) [1]

A group of ladies conversed as their needles poked in and out of a quilt needing to be finished before summer's end. Two mothers were interrupted occasionally by their young children. One listened carefully to each request or complaint and then quietly offered an answer or stopped quilting in order to solve a problem. The other mother easily brushed her children aside before they had finished speaking. "I'm quilting now; run along and play. Just get along with the others and don't fuss." She continued quilting dutifully in Martha fashion, but her children called for a Mary heart. So does the Lord.

"Martha, Martha," Jesus chided gently, "thou art careful and troubled about many things: but one thing is needful: and Mary hath chosen that good part, which shall not be taken away from her" (see Luke 10:41, 42).

Martha's work is not wrong. What daughter of Eve hasn't struggled with knowing what to prioritize and what to eliminate? Guests should be fed and quilts should be finished, but balancing our work with our relationships to God and others is crucial.

How easy it is to weaken our effectiveness in passing

faith along by being industriously or selfishly consumed in our Martha work at the expense of our Mary heart. Quickly that which is urgent chases away that which is eternally important. Our challenge is to be faithful while we complete our urgent tasks and determine to set them aside for time at Jesus' feet.

Sometimes our Mary heart has to come back to the kitchen and the Martha work that waits so that our families are not left frustrated and continually inconvenienced. At the same time, families can learn to sacrifice so that mothers can answer the call to prolonged worship.

Balancing between Martha's world and Mary's heart will be a lifelong challenge for all daughters of God.

Sturdily Stacking

God recommended heaping stones as sturdy reminders. When the children of Israel crossed the Jordan River to claim the promised land, God told Joshua: "Take you twelve men . . . and command . . . them, saying, Take you hence out of the midst of Jordan . . . twelve stones, and ye shall carry them over with you, and leave them in the lodging place, where ye shall lodge this night" (Joshua 4:2, 3).

Why? "That this may be a sign among you, that when your children ask their fathers in time to come, saying, What mean ye by these stones? Then ye shall answer them, That the waters of Jordan were cut off before the ark of the covenant of the LORD; when it passed over Jordan, the waters of Jordan were cut off: and these stones shall be for a memorial unto the children of Israel for ever" (Joshua 4:6, 7).

The twelve stones the men lifted from the riverbed were carried to where the children of Israel camped in

Gilgal. There Joshua set them up as a reminder to teach the children what had happened. Not only would future generations of children marvel at the miracle God performed that day, but when the kings of the land heard about the dried-up waters of the Jordan, "their heart[s] melted" in fear (Joshua 5:1). It was obvious that this nation had a God who cared about them immensely. God's unmatched strength was manifested in their deliverance. "That all the people of the earth might know the hand of the LORD, that it is mighty: that ye might fear the LORD your God for ever" (Joshua 4:24).

"What stones can I stack?" I asked God. These are the answers He gave me as I meditated on what might prompt our children to ask questions:

1. **Erect altars.** Each time families gather for family worship, another stone is added to an important altar. This very important stack of stones anchors a child through many of life's storms. It provides an underlying firmness on which children can begin to build a personal altar of worship.

2. **Gather nuggets of truth.** The Scriptures are filled with golden nuggets that fit easily into the pocket of one's heart. Throughout the day they can be gripped while facing a challenge, or admired while meditating. Gather nuggets for yourself and the children in your world. "Therefore shall ye lay up these my words in your heart and in your soul, and bind them for a sign upon your hand . . . . And ye shall teach them your children, speaking of them when thou sittest in thine house, and when thou walkest by the way, when thou liest down, and when thou risest up . . . that your days may be multiplied, and the days of your children" (Deuteronomy 11:18-21).

3. **Find clefts of prayer.** Pray with and for your children. A mother's prayers are known to have a tremendous effect on a person's life, but this responsibility does not rest with mothers alone. Blessed is the father, the teacher, the aunt, the mentor, the person who cares enough to pray for — and with — a child. "Arise, cry out in the night: in the beginning of the watches pour out thine heart like water before the face of the LORD: lift up thy hands toward him for the life of thy young children" (Lamentations 2:19).

4. **Build your marriage.** Tear down walls that separate you from your husband. If he is unwilling to help, run to your Tower of Strength and pray faithfully. Build each other up. Respect your spouse; model it before your children. Remember that your marriage paints a picture of Christ's love for the church.

5. **Be careful about building your church.** First Corinthians 3:10-12 speaks of different materials: gold, silver, precious stones, wood, hay, stubble. "But let every man take heed how he buildeth thereupon"(verse 10). Building on the foundation of Christ, church members are challenged toward works that will not burn in fire. Strive to be more than dead wood or easily ignited hay or stubble in your church.

6. **Lay up blessings at bedtime.** Is it the reflective quality in the close of a day that opens one's heart

to communication? Other mothers have also discovered that children—even those who resist talking about things—are more apt to share verbally just before sleep. There is no law that says tucking children into bed must stop by age five. Kneeling beside a child's bed in prayer is a privilege. On occasion I like to lay my hand on a drowsy forehead and pray a prayer of blessing on my child. There may come stages in life when our children resist that, at least in word, but I suspect the heart longs for it. In the words of our youngest child, "I feel all empty when no one tucks me in."

We must be careful to respect our children's desires as they mature; but a mother can always ask: "May I tuck you in tonight?" "May I pray with you?"

Mothers may echo the sentiments of Apostle Paul and his helpers in 1 Thessalonians 2:7, 8: "But we were gentle among you, even as a nurse cherisheth her children: So being affectionately desirous of you, we were willing to have imparted unto you, not the gospel of God only, but also our own souls, because ye were dear unto us."

 7. Stack stones for practical guidance. Scripture verses displayed prominently in our homes, godly music, modest dress and walk of life, simple and peaceful homes, obedience to Scriptures—all can be stacks of stones that help us and our children to walk on in faith. "The secret things belong unto the LORD our God: but those things which are revealed belong unto us and to our children for ever, that we may do all the words of this law" (Deuteronomy 29:29). Practical stacks of stones help to guide us and our children on the narrow way.

The July sun beat on the massive red rock that stretched before us, angling upward for many yards to a maze of rock pillars and formations in the distance. My husband and I and our children had already hiked over a half mile in the 103-degree heat. Now the trail vanished. Not a single footprint marked the solid stone. Somewhere out there in the intriguing Utah beauty of Arches National Park stood the Delicate Arch—our destination.

Scanning the rock before us, we saw them—small stacks of stones, placed at intervals across the massive rock, marking the path we and other park visitors were to take. "Upon reaching the slick rock, follow the rock cairns." We remembered the instructions at the beginning of our trek where the trail was well-worn and easily defined.

We started our climb, carefully rationing our water. Several of the children ran ahead. Before long one of them was sprawled on the rock, threatening to climb no farther. With encouragement from the rest of the family and a refreshing drink of water, the resistant adolescent rejoined our desert hike. Eventually we rounded a massive tower of rock to view the famous arch perched delicately at the brink of a huge crater. With awe we took pleasure in the landscape and carefully climbed along sloping rock to stand beneath the lofty arch.

The water lasted just long enough to refresh our one-and-a-half-mile journey back to the parking lot, where we congratulated ourselves on our accomplishment. Our family never forgot the beauty we viewed that day or the effort we expended to capture it.

As my own reminiscent stack of stones, I later

ordered personal checks decorated with scenes from nature. Now each time I write a check over the picture of the Delicate Arch, I am reminded of a time when our family persisted in following stacks of stones to a desired destination. To me it is a reminder to pass faith along to my children so that they can reach the ultimate destination — Heaven.

In whatever way you are called to minister to children, use your opportunities to pass along faith. Dry their tears with Scriptures of hope. Tuck them in with a blessing. And stack stones that will lead them through the deserts of their lives.

Be careful when you stack stones. Children will ask questions!

Scriptures

"[Joshua] spake unto the children of Israel, saying,
When your children shall ask their fathers
in time to come, saying,
What mean these stones?
Then ye shall let your children know."
Joshua 4:21-22

"O thou afflicted, tossed with tempest . . .
behold, I will lay thy stones with fair colours,
and lay thy foundations with sapphires . . .
and all thy borders of pleasant stones.
And all thy children shall be taught of the LORD;
and great shall be the peace of thy children."
Isaiah 54:11-13

"I have set before you life and death,
blessing and cursing:
therefore choose life,
that both thou and thy seed may live:
That thou mayest love the LORD thy God,
and that thou mayest obey his voice,
and that thou mayest cleave unto him:
for he is thy life, and the length of thy days."
Deuteronomy 30: 19, 20

Prayer

Dear Father,

According to Your direction, I want to be faithful in passing faith along to the next generations.

Help me to display a vibrant, winsome faith, a careful faith. When my own faith is challenged and chased, remind me to walk away from my Martha's world to sit at your feet with a Mary's heart.

Help me to stack stones sturdily in ways that will prompt children to ask questions. Give me answers from Your Word. Let me not be afraid to tether Scriptures to a child's world by personal testimony of Your faithfulness.

Oh, Father, let us raise the family altar of worship higher for Your glory. Help me to build in our home, tearing down only when walls separate. Let my works be of gold, silver, and precious stones rather than wood, hay, or stubble so that our church will be strong for oncoming generations. Strengthen me in prayer; give me the desire to pray with and for my children. Help them to be accepting of bedtime blessings.

Especially help me to honor Your Word, to be obedient to Your commands, and to be ever mindful of Your kingdom . . .

. . . Until You Come Again,

CHAPTER 12

Teachers of Good Things

*A*lthough I was only a teenager, I vividly recall the feelings that stirred within me when I entered the small, upstairs apartment. With typical youthful gusto, I had joined several other teenagers painting a church building for a small group of church-planting believers in another state. One day I went with some girls to the home of a young church family for some needed items.

"Come in," called a cheery voice in answer to our knock. The scent of freshly laundered clothes burst upon us as we opened the door. Zigzagged across the small kitchen and living room were wash lines full of drying laundry. A pleasant face emerged from a row of diapers.

"Join me over here," the young mother called as she parted a path through the laundry with one hand and balanced a spoonful of baby cereal with the other. I doubt she realized as she sat spooning cereal into the eager little mouth that she was setting an example for me. I stole laundry-blocked glances around the simple apartment. Not once did Phyllis apologize for its appearance. Calmly she continued feeding her baby while she chatted, thanking us for our work in their community. She spoke of their outreach and sense of mission. I left that apartment with a picture of contented commitment that I have not forgotten. One young mother taught a younger daughter of God the importance of serving family, living simply, and reaching out to the community. I did not know that one day I would have the opportunity to return the favor.

Twenty years later I was singing in the morning sun as I hung laundry on my wash line. Suddenly a hand parted the laundry and a smiling face emerged. The friendly face was grown-up now, but it belonged to the baby that was being fed in that apartment long ago. Rose and I greeted each other warmly. Visiting her grandparents next door, she had heard me singing and came to say hello. Extending her arm toward the shady porch where a row of simply made dresses swayed on hangers, she said with a smile, "It looks like a dress shop." Her next comment warmed my heart. "You make homemaking look like so much fun."

She asked about our move to town and what had prompted it. I spoke of our desire to serve the church in practical ways and to be ambassadors for Christ in our community. With a wave of warm satisfaction, I realized I was setting an example for this young daughter of God in the same simple way her mother had taught me.

According to Titus 2:3-5 daughters of God are expected to be teachers. Being "teachers of good things" blesses women with a sense of fulfillment and blesses the women being taught with a sense of purpose. With or without trying, you are teaching the women around you. Why not put effort into guiding others in paths of peace and purpose?

Teaching and Mentoring

Women have been teaching each other since Eve gave the first sewing, cooking, and "submission" classes to her descendants. Through the generations that followed, women have taught women the skills of womanhood. But beyond the many necessary skills needed to prepare, preserve, replenish, replace, revitalize, discipline, nourish, and nurture, women can mentor other women and children in hungering after God.

A mentor is defined as a wise or trusted teacher or counselor. A mentor teaches—sometimes in formal, or at least scheduled, ways and sometimes in more informal ways—and displays an attractive example to those who follow in her footsteps.

A beautiful part of aging is remembering how others mentored us and reaching out in turn to mentor others. "The aged women likewise, that they be in behaviour as becometh holiness, . . . teachers of good things" (Titus 2:3). Before you let the word "aged" silence you, consider that some women are younger than you.

Have you walked down a certain path and now see another woman taking similar steps? That path has aged you; you can offer her sips of the spiritual refreshment you received along the way. Do not hide the truths you have learned. Befriend younger women or babes in Christ. Affirm them. Pray for—and with— them. Identify with, and speak gracefully to, their needs.

Are you a young woman? Or new to the narrow way? Do not be afraid to tap into the rich resource of godly women who surround you. Ask them questions. Observe their attitudes toward life. Humble yourself and verbalize your need of advice or mentoring.

I am encouraged when I see women seeking and sharing wisdom. Together we can pore over the Bible or exchange practical advice. Recently I overheard a conversation:

"How do you get Nicole to sit so still in church? Our daughter is at the age where she wants to wiggle and throw things."

"Oh, she doesn't always sit still."

"She does very well, though, especially for her age."

"Well, there is one thing I do. Actually, I learned it from an experienced mother in my home congregation. She said she would read to her toddler every day; while she was reading, the child had to sit still and listen to the story. I've tried to do that. It is a pleasant way of helping Nicole learn to sit still."

"What a good idea! I'm going to try that. Lena is just beginning to enjoy books."

Give and receive good teaching, as these mothers did, by taking these steps: Look for other women whose values and faithfulness you admire. Ask them questions. When you ask, allow yourself to be vulnerable; let the other know you have weaknesses and are in need of help. Listen to and consider their advice. Put it into practice. Evaluate the results. Share what you have learned with others as you have opportunity.

Finding Mentors

Years ago I went on a mentor hunt. Quietly I observed women, listened to their testimonies, and critiqued their faith. I tested the waters, putting one great toe of my need into the pool of their friendship. If the water was hot (scolding and discouraging), I recoiled. If the water was cold (distant), or lukewarm (just that), I tried elsewhere. Where the water was warm and welcoming I waded in up to my knees. With a few "kindred spirits" I dived right in and delighted in their warm guidance and encouragement. (After a dive like that I love to sit on the shore of God's kindness and watch the ripples of friendship widen and swell.)

I am grateful for a variety of teachers and mentors. Some of them teach me about parenting; a few have provided specific guidance for foster and adoptive parenting. I have organization mentors, poetry mentors, and homemaking mentors, but my favorite ones double (or triple) as my spiritual mentors as well. These women provide loving guidance for me in my areas of need. I have learned to listen for their cues: "I have found . . ." "I am learning to . . ." "This Bible verse helps me . . ."

Do my mentors offer only pleasant encouragement? No. Sometimes I need their gentle rebukes, quiet reminders, and loaded questions.

"What is the truth about this situation?" one especially insightful mentor occasionally asks me when I am dodging the devil's darts of self-condemning thoughts. Often she helps me look honestly at circumstances or situations that I have distorted in my mind. I will admit there are times I want to jump out of this kind of encounter, shake myself off like a dog, and run away with my tail between my legs. But I have learned the truth of Proverbs 27:6: "Faithful are the wounds of a friend." I readily acknowledge that much of my growth in character as a daughter of God has been prompted by spiritual mentors who have listened while I cried, encouraged repentance, cited promises from God's Word, and offered prayers on my behalf. I owe a continuing debt of gratitude to each of them.

A young woman was eager to learn from women older than she was. She asked to be part of a women's

Sunday school class of mixed ages; the variety in age and perspective attracted her. In seeking help from mature women, this young woman opened doors and invited others to be her mentors. Each class member benefited from her search. Joy said, "I appreciate the guidance of these older sisters; we can learn so much from them!" Sadie said, "I enjoy having the younger sisters in our class, they add so much—and keep us challenged!" As the years passed, the members of the class attended funerals. "We are going down the valley one by one," they sang at yet another funeral one Saturday. On Sunday morning the teacher commented on the truth of the song for their smaller class. One by one the older women of the class were mentoring the younger women in how to travel the last mile of the way.

Do you wish for spiritual mentors, friends who pray with you, open their Bibles to point out trusted verses, and guide you in paths of peace? Begin by praying for one (or more than one). Bring the desires of your heart to God and ask Him to provide women who can minister to your areas of need. Watch women whose faith attracts you. It may be out of character for you, but consider straightforwardly asking someone to mentor you.

While seeking a mentor, ask questions (evidence of a desire to learn), and be transparent (evidence of a desire to be vulnerable and honest about yourself). A woman who has walked humbly with God through paths checkered by shade and sunshine will most likely be honored to mentor you. Thank her for being a Titus 2 woman.

Learning from Mothers

Mothers and mothers-in-law are often some of our

closest teachers and mentors. We may go to them with questions that we would be embarrassed to ask anyone else.

I remember one time when I especially needed a mother's advice. It was late in the evening and I was preparing syrup for my "seven-day pickles" after being away from home for most of the day. As I started to measure the vinegar into my saucepan, a strange, slimy film appeared in the neck of the bottle. *What is the matter with my vinegar?*

I glanced with dismay at the clock. It was too late to go to the store for more. Otherwise the vinegar looked and smelled fine. *Should I use it?* I phoned my mother-in-law and explained my problem. Her warm chuckle sounded in my ear. "Oh, that's mother," she said.

"*Mother?*" I queried.

"Yes, mother of vinegar. It grows in vinegar sometimes. Just pour that away. It's okay to use the rest of it." I sighed with relief but could not contain my curiosity.

"Why do they call it 'mother'?" I asked, incredulous. Again she chuckled. Together we decided that maybe it was called that because every young cook has to ask her mother what it is. I am uncertain what advice a licensed dietitian would give me regarding mother in my vinegar, but on that evening I gladly listened to the advice of my other mother.

I discovered later that, if I had known the name of it, I could have found the definition in my dictionary, for indeed it is there. Go ahead, look it up—or ask your mother about it.

My friend Trudy speaks reverently about the mentoring she received from her mother-in-law. Her own mother died before Trudy's tenth birthday, and she was raised by a busy father and his elderly parents. In young adulthood, Trudy met and married a man from a Mennonite home. The faith and ways of her in-law's family fascinated her. She was ripe for mentoring. She says:

Even though our backgrounds were so different, Barbara and I had a common bond—she had lost her mother to death at the age of seven. She knew what it was like to be passed around from home to home before she finally had a home of her own. Barbara could have labeled me an "outsider" and treated me as such, but she never did. She took me under her wing and patiently answered my questions. She confided in me, allowing me to see her vulnerable side and sharing some of her struggles with me.

I could feel her prayers. Not in a condescending way that said "you should be like I am," but in a way that made me feel genuinely loved. Her prayers and attitude toward me communicated that she wanted what was best for me. She did not give up on me, even when I gave her reason to. Her mentoring guided me in embracing the faith to which I'd been attracted.

While reviewing this manuscript, I accepted a new role; I became a grandmother! How gladly I answered my daughter's request. "I don't know a lot about caring for newborns," LaNell said, "but I would like my mom to teach me."

Precious days were spent teaching and affirming my daughter and cuddling our grandson. Living nearby, LaNell's mother-in-law also blessed her with help and advice. What a thrill for a mother to feel the softness of a grandchild's cheek against her own and know that she can continue to teach—and reach another generation!

Sometimes mothers and mothers-in-law are far away and the new bride or new mother feels alone. "Don't be afraid to ask other women for help and advice," I tell my daughter Lori as she prepares to marry and move thousands of miles away. I yearn to help her as she begins homemaking. Phone calls, letters, and packages go a long way, but I know that she will need the support and mentoring of other women.

Mother and mother-in-law, gracefully accept the opportunity to teach or mentor but do not step beyond your place. Be available. Be a good example. Listen. Teach in tender, non-threatening ways. Give affirmation. And when we blunder, "I'm sorry" teaches too.

Me Mentor?

Does the thought of mentoring others frighten you? Accept the challenge. Have you asked, as I have, "Where do I begin?" And "How can I be certain to give good advice?" Again Titus 2 provides guidance. The good things listed for us to teach are "to be sober, to love their husbands, to love their children, to be discreet, chaste, keepers at home, good, obedient to their own husbands." We need to be certain our mentoring does not contradict these guidelines. A non-threatening place to begin teaching these good things is in our homes to our young daughters or siblings, being mindful that example teaches more effectively than words.

We may begin by teaching and training children in the fundamentals of godly womanhood, keeping house, and yes, even things as simple as what to do when encountering mother of vinegar. But on the shores of our faith laps another wave that would call us out to sea — the sea of reaching out.

"But sanctify the Lord God in your hearts: and be ready always to give an answer to every man that asketh you a reason of the hope that is in you with meekness and fear" (1 Peter 3:15). Daughters of God can be *ready always* to provide answers filled with *hope!* The hope of salvation. The hope of God's Word and His promises. The hope of growing in grace. We have so much hope to offer those whom the devil has snared in hopelessness. Christ's commission in Acts 1:8 is a charge to sons and daughters of God. We, as women, can rise to the call of being spiritual mentors to other women.

Effective Spiritual Mentoring

- *Knowing Jesus Christ.* The most important factor in becoming an effective spiritual mentor is to know — really know — Christ. Know Him as sovereign Lord, as trusted Saviour, as intimate Friend. Knowing Him will enable us: "According as his divine power hath given unto us all things that pertain unto life and godliness, through the knowledge of him that hath called us to glory and virtue: whereby are given unto us exceeding great and precious promises" (2 Peter 1:3, 4).

- *Cultivating an Interest in People.* The second step is to cultivate an interest in people. Ask God to give you a heart that cares about the joys and struggles of other women. Review and praise God's kindness to you. Recognize His work in the lives of others. Ask God to remove your fear of reaching out to that troubled teen, the woman whose marriage is floundering, or the unsaved neighbor who asks you questions about your faith. Dare to care. Care enough to share. Lead them to your Father.

- *Examining Biblical Mentors.* A third step is to examine Biblical accounts of women who mentored. Consider Anna the prophetess and Elisabeth the mother of John. Anna, widowed for eighty-four years and serving God daily in the temple, was blessed with the privilege of meeting Baby Jesus when His parents brought Him to the temple. What did she do? She gave thanks to God, "and spake of him to all them that looked for redemption in Jerusalem" (Luke 2:38). She did not stay silent about the Ray of Hope she knew would provide light for those who sought.

  When the angel announced to Mary that she would bear God's Son, he hinted of a place she could go to be encouraged and mentored. "And, behold, thy cousin Elisabeth, she hath also conceived a son in her old age" (Luke 1:36). Can you imagine Mary going "with haste" (Luke 1:39) to the house of Zacharias and Elisabeth? She needed a mentor, someone to stand beside her and confirm the things she had been told, someone to teach and train her in the surprising ways of God. It was after Elisabeth's greeting and blessing — and unborn John's as well — that Mary burst into the lovely praises of the Magnificat recorded in Luke 1:46-56. For three months Mary absorbed her older cousin's mentoring. What a precious, beneficial gift from their Lord!

  Phebe, "a servant of the church," is commended

by Apostle Paul in Romans 16:1, 2. We do not know what her help for Paul and many others involved, but she may well have taught other women important aspects of servanthood.

- *Resting in God's Leading.* Fourth, daughters of God can rest in the leading of the Lord regarding the teaching of good things. Mentoring does not have to be scheduled, formal, or profound. It can happen spontaneously when doing something as routine as making a meal. For instance, I telephoned a special mentor of mine this afternoon. I thanked her for guiding and encouraging me over the past ten years. Today she is making oyster stew. "I'm taking it to a dear friend who is dying of cancer and can hardly swallow," she said. Without fanfare or volumes of advice, my friend, through her actions, taught me about priorities.

  Sometimes scheduling more formal mentoring is helpful. For a period of months I had the opportunity to meet weekly with a young daughter of God. My painful past paled in comparison to hers, but she had been watching my journey of healing and asked for help. Our bond of friendship strengthened as together we gloried in being daughters of God even while we struggled at times as daughters of Eve. We pored over God's Word and claimed His promises. "Let us search and try our ways, and turn again to the LORD. Let us lift up our heart with our hands unto God in the heavens." Our desire was echoed in Lamentations 3:40, 41. As we lifted up our hearts with our hands before the Lord, we found that His mercies were still saving, His compassions still new every morning, His faithfulness still great—we had hope (see Lamentations 3:21-26).

- *Treasuring God's Word.* Making Scripture your primary guide in mentoring is a fifth important step in being effective. Books abound that offer help in overcoming and moving forward in hope, but the Book is still the source of all hope. Treasure it enough to share its truths. Let the Bible be your guide in choosing other helpful resources. Ask yourself and someone you trust, "Is it Biblical?"

- *Bathe Your Mentoring in Prayer.* Pray before, after, and while you teach. "Lord, I do not know how to help this daughter of Yours. Give me insight and understanding. I need Your wisdom." God is faithful. He will hear and help as we seek.

Package With Care

Packaging and delivery are important parts of teaching and mentoring. Do we hammer a truth home, heedless of the person's feelings? God asks us to put the hammer away and gift-wrap our teaching. Second Peter 1:5-7 offers an array of lovely wrappings. Wrap your mentoring in diligence, virtue, self-control, and patience. Package knowledge, godliness, brotherly kindness, and charity inside the wrappings. "For if these things be in you, and abound, they make you that ye shall neither be barren nor unfruitful in the knowledge of our Lord Jesus Christ" (2 Peter 1:8). Other women are apt to relish your mentoring when you have carefully gift-wrapped it per God's instructions.

Mind Our Motives

Even the best actions may be driven by less than righteous motives. Hiding behind a desire to teach or mentor others may be an ungodly desire to prove my worth or elevate myself. We blush—rightfully so—at our selfish daughter-of-Eve motives. Sincerely checking those motives may be soul-wrenching, but it can be followed by soul-cleansing. "Examine me, O LORD, and prove me: try my reins and my heart" (Psalm 26:2). God can and will forgive and *remotivate* repentant daughters of God.

Use me, O Lord, to teach and mentor other women for Thy glory rather than my own. Our Father's heart is touched by simple contrite prayers. The soul that seeks to glorify God is fit for the Master's use.

This Is the Path

Mentoring. I love the sound of the word. It has a coming-alongside ring to it. A gentle, loving "This is the path, now walk ye in it" message. Receive it. Pass it along to others. Give mentoring a chance to help you grow.

Teaching does not come easily for everyone; some are gifted in other ways. But each daughter of God can mentor—walk alongside someone, teaching by word and example— when, where, and how she feels comfortable. Until one day God will call her beyond her comfort zone. "Will you be my spiritual mentor?" asks a young woman in the church foyer. "Will you pray with me?" asks a troubled Christian. "Can you answer my questions?" asks a new believer.

And the daughter of God can answer—with full assurance in her Father—"Of course I will."

Scriptures

"For God hath not given us the spirit of fear;
but of power, and of love, and of a sound mind."
2 Timothy 1:7

"Study to shew thyself approved unto God,
a workman that needeth not to be ashamed,
rightly dividing the word of truth."
2 Timothy 2:15

"Wherefore also we pray always for you,
that our God would count you
worthy of this calling, and fulfill all
the good pleasure of his goodness,
and the work of faith with power:
that the name of our Lord Jesus Christ
may be glorified in you,
and ye in him, according to the grace of our God
and the Lord Jesus Christ."
2 Thessalonians 1:11, 12

Prayer

Dear Father,

Give me a humble, teachable heart – one that is willing to receive teaching and mentoring from other women.

Give me a grateful, caring heart – one that is willing to teach and mentor other women.

Give me confidence in You. Help me to learn more about You. Let Your Word be my guide and trusted companion. Help me to lean on You in prayer and gift-wrap teaching and mentoring according to Your instructions.

Thank you for women who mentor me. Bless them for being Titus 2 women.

Gratefully,

CHAPTER 13

Reaching Beyond

"May I . . . ask a question?" stammered the service station attendant in faltering English.

"Sure," I said with a smile.

"Are you . . . uh . . . Jewish? Catholic?" He nodded toward my veiled head.

"No, I am Mennonite."

"Ah, yes, Menn-o-nite." He motioned out the window. "Many Mennonites come, stop here for gas. I wonder . . . what you believe?" His dark eyes mirrored true interest. A work-worn brown hand tapped his chest. "I Indian . . . from India . . . I can know what you believe?"

"Yes. I know of some Mennonites in India . . ."

"In India, yes?" The attendant's eyebrows jumped upward.

"Some missionaries, yes." Then, not wanting to miss the more important question, and thinking fleetingly of the fact that this discussion may make me late to pick up my daughter some distance away, I breathed a quick prayer before I continued. *Lord, here is a soul that needs You. Help me give him a glowing glimpse of You as I answer his questions. You know about the time. I'll give him some tracts too; help them convey more of the message to his heart.*

"Mennonites are Christians," I began, pronouncing my words carefully. "We believe the Bible. It is God's Book to man—every man. We believe in Jesus. We believe that He is also God and that He came to earth as a baby, grew to be a man to show us how to live, and died on a cross to save us from our sins." I paused, thrilled with the truth I was sharing and for the opportunity to share with this man. "After three days, Jesus rose from the dead—He became *alive again!* Jesus is in Heaven with God, and because of what He did for me, I can go to Heaven to live with God forever when I die." I offered him the tracts. "These will tell you more. You, too, can have Jesus for a friend. He can be your God."

The attendant reached eagerly for the tracts, turning them over in his hand. "Yes, thank you, thank you." He pointed to the Mennonites depicted on the front of one of the tracts. "Now I read what you believe." He smiled and thanked me again.

Back in the car, I could not suppress the song of praise that rose from my bubbling heart. Before, I had been complaining to myself about having to make the long drive alone for the second time in one week; now I marveled at how God had placed me in the path of a searching soul. As I frequently do, I reached to touch my covering, feeling for any dents that needed to be straightened. *Thank You, Lord, for the privilege of wearing this headship veiling. It affords me so many opportunities to share my beliefs and tell others about You!* I glanced at my watch. *Lord, I took time to speak for You. Will you please take care of my time for arrival?*

Two hours later, after repentance for my bad attitude, praise for a changed attitude, and rich worship of my Lord, I stepped out of the car—just in time to meet my daughter.

God gives His daughters opportunities to reach beyond their family circles and tell others about Him. With a faith so rich, a Hell to escape, and a secure hope for a blissful eternity, how can we be silent?

Whom Can I Reach?

Daughters of God have a message of joy: "You can be a child of God. You can learn from His chastening. You can treasure His cherishing. You can rise to His challenging." Whom can we tell?

Our own children, or children in our care, rank as first priority. We dare not underestimate the importance of reaching them. But we may teach those very children to have a heart for others by ministering to the needs of others ourselves. Of course we can minister to the people in our churches; but to demonstrate a greater compassion for lost souls we must be concerned about our neighbors, people we meet, and yes, even the Jehovah's Witness or salesman at the door.

If you earnestly desire to reach beyond (the Great Commission tells us we will), pray about it. Opportunities abound; it is our awareness that needs to be heightened and our responses that need to be enhanced.

Step out of your personal world and look around you. The elderly woman next door may soon enter eternity. Does she know Jesus as her personal Saviour? Young children playing in your neighborhood may delight in visiting the peace and safety of your home. Do you dare give them a glimpse? The rowdy boys up the road may seem to have missed their share of spankings.

Have you surprised them by showing concern for them? Do you acknowledge that unkempt family in the community with respect or with scorn? Do we shrink in fear (or disgust) from the opportunities God places before us?

Dan visited a place of business frequently. All of the employees claimed to be born-again Christians. "But Dan is a fearsome fellow," they said. "If only he would clean up a bit, or shave, or dress differently." Some tried to reach out to Dan. They invited him to church and he came. But when Dan learned that some of the employees did not like him invading their territory he mumbled, "If Christians are like that, I don't need them, and I won't come back." What Dan really needed was a personal, life-changing relationship with Christ. How sad that he felt rejection from Christ's followers.

"But we need to be careful whom we are dealing with," anxious Christians declare. True. We must exercise caution; women especially need to show Christian modesty as commanded in 1 Timothy 2:9. At the same time, people who do not fit our picture of Christianity are not necessarily hardened criminals to be feared.

Are we willing to risk reaching beyond our circles of comfort? Religious leaders criticized Jesus when He ate with sinners and tax collectors. "They that are whole have no need of the physician, but they that are sick: I came not to call the righteous, but sinners to repentance," Jesus replied in Mark 2:17. Are there times He would reprove us in the same way? Have our fears and concerns crippled our witness?

As it turned out, the husband and wife Glen and Cora reached out to were criminal material. For months, four or more couples from church assisted Glen and Cora in helping the struggling mother and her young children. The father reentered the picture and efforts were made to lead the troubled pair to a saving knowledge of Christ. Rather than improving, problems mushroomed. Eventually the man was incarcerated for a horrendous crime, and the woman returned to a life of sin. Glen and Cora and their friends mourned for the couple. They grieved for the children whose lives were so warped by the poor decisions of their parents. *What should we have done differently? Should we have reached out to them at all? Were our efforts futile?* Seeking answers for their own questions, the Christian couples learned valuable lessons: It was not wrong to reach out. Seeds had been planted, and although they appeared to have been trampled, the harvest rested in God's realm. One day those seeds could sprout and grow, even if it seemed unlikely. God had protected Glen and Cora and their friends in the face of danger, and they had learned a lot about setting boundaries when reaching out. God provided a concerned brother from a neighboring church to continue visiting the man in prison. The marriage crumbled and the woman spurned the ways of God. Some time later, Cora met some of the children. Their eyes still sparkled at the memory of people who cared enough to try to help. Despite the disturbing results, God's name could still be glorified.

Witnessing is not always surrounded by fears and frustrations. Sometimes it is surprisingly easy and pleasant. "Do you have a personal relationship with Christ?" I asked a visitor to our church. DeeDee pondered my question as she pored over the tracts she had picked up from the tract rack. Days later her soul found rest as she read about the Romans road to salvation. "I'd never been asked that question before," DeeDee related. "But the more I thought about it, the more I knew that is what I wanted."

Witnessing to lost souls is not the only way to reach

out to others. There are new Christians to be discipled, mature Christians to be encouraged, and erring brothers and sisters to meekly restore to faith.

Look around you. The fields really are ripe to harvest. Even now some fields that have not known the sweet sound of the sickle are teeming with waiting souls while governments try to keep doors shut to the Gospel. But God's Word will not return void; in places where Christianity has been repressed, the underground church is growing mightily. Maybe you or I can go. Maybe we are busy raising or teaching a child who will go. Wherever we are, wherever we may go, there are people who need to hear.

How Can I Reach?

"I can't speak very well." "I don't know what to say." "I get all nervous when I try to talk to someone about Christ." Believers are hampered by excuses. We serve a God who created our tongues and redeemed our lives. How can we doubt His ability to use us to witness for Him?

Concerned about their supposed inadequacies, some Christians overlook a most important witnessing tool — one's smile. Try it. When you go to the grocery store, the doctor's office, a restaurant, the post office, or even a public restroom — smile. But don't just smile at the floor, the wall, or the mirror. Look into the eyes of people and smile. Eye contact and a pleasant facial expression tell people it is okay to ask questions about my faith. I have often been asked about the significance of my headship veiling when I have invited people to ask — by simply smiling.

Observe people in public, especially in small settings where strangers stand next to each other or face people they do not know. Ride the hospital elevator and count how many people look at the floor, at the ceiling, or anything other than the faces of the people riding with them. Try a simple experiment. Look into the eyes of your fellow elevator riders, smile, and say, "Hello." Strike up a simple conversation or wait for them to respond to you. In either case you have completed the first leg of a journey that just may lead to an opportunity to share Christ. No, I am not suggesting you ride hospital elevators for hours of witnessing. (You could try it; it just might be effective. Then again you might be interrogated or asked to leave the premises.) Make a pleasant face—with an invitation to conversation—a part of your normal appearance in public. You may be surprised how opening a door in this small way will bless you with opportunities to reach beyond.

Be pleasant, but not plastic. Feign pleasantness when you are hurting, and you miss the opportunity to be real. People will perceive you as fake and won't see the value of God's grace in your present suffering. After my father had had several strokes, our family was grieved at the effects. I escaped to the garden one day for a brief respite from caregiving. A neighbor stopped to chat, unaware of the difficulties we faced. I found myself honestly sharing about the anguish I was experiencing, but crediting our endurance to God's grace. Quickly and freely my neighbor began talking about her struggles with a bitter parent. Being pleasant is not the only way to point souls to Jesus.

"But I am not comfortable talking with strangers or neighbors," one may say. Understandably not everyone is a born communicator. God has given believers a variety of gifts. You may be an interested listener. (Think of the many people in our busy world who love to be listened to.) You may be a giver or a doer of good works. You may witness about Christ through your holy life. Sometimes the old adage applies to witnessing: Actions speak louder than words. Do those things that come easily for you—the things that fit best with your personality. But do not shut doors that God wishes to open for you, and do not be surprised if God calls you beyond your comfort zone.

People who seem to resist hearing you speak about Christ may gratefully receive your alms and learn of Christ's love in practical ways. Seeds are planted in this way as well. "To the MenaNights" reads a thank-you note on our church bulletin board. It continues: "Thank you to the people who were generous enough to give us the food that you people gave us!!" The carefully formed letters are those of a child from a needy family. The practical help may not answer the need of their souls, but it may help them to hunger in a deeper way.

Writing letters is another way to reach beyond to searching souls. What began as a tourist asking questions about the Mennonites has led to an interesting exchange of letters between me and a young Christian who lives over a thousand miles away. Both of us have learned a lot about answers from the Bible. I have saved a number of letters from a ninety-year-old widow who wanted to encourage me in the Lord. Age did not stop her from reaching out to others. A new believer tells how a card of encouragement that she received in the mail was just what she needed to strengthen her in the battle against the enemy. "He wants me back, but people care and I am going to cling even harder to Jesus." Is the Lord asking you to write a letter?

Handing out Gospel tracts can be an effective way to witness. One rarely knows just how people are affected or how many lives are changed through tract distribution. Beware of doing it as a comfortable way to witness while spurning other options. Easing your conscience by dropping a tract at someone's door and then hurrying away may leave that person wishing he could have asked you some questions.

A daughter of God may stay at home all day and witness to the ones within her home and the ones who come to the door. Or a daughter of God may go, answering a call to serve as an ambassador for Christ in a faraway city or the closest grocery store. Stay or go, but as you do, sow, sow, sow.

"And God is able to make all grace abound toward you; that ye, always having all sufficiency in all things, may abound to every good work: now he that ministereth seed to the sower both minister bread for your food, and multiply your seed sown, and increase the fruits of your righteousness" (2 Corinthians 9:8, 10).

What Can I Do to Reach Effectively?

Probably one of the most effective ways for a woman to *reach beyond* is to faithfully *stay within*. What message do I convey if I stay within God's will for me? Staying within the boundaries of my marriage, my home, and my church, staying faithful to serving my family — staying within demonstrates faith in God. A faithful wife and mother with a happy, contented countenance is a real witness in a world of discontent! Even something as simple as singing at the wash line gives an important message to children, neighbors, or passersby: *I am content to stay where God graciously led me.*

Another effective way to reach out is to be an encourager. Encouragers do not have to be gifted speakers or profound advisers; rather they know the right time to use encouraging words or actions. "The devil seems determined to get our family back," a dear friend told me with a hug. "You and your husband have been such an encouragement to us, and—praise the Lord—we are experiencing victory." While my friend thanked us for being encouragers, we felt encouraged by their newfound faith and commitment to spiritual growth. Encouragement is like that: it blesses the giver and the receiver.

Effective reaching out happens when we are willing to disciple new believers or mentor other believers. Discipleship takes time, effort, and a long-range focus. Some of us may not feel comfortable with evangelism, but encouragers and teachers are just as necessary for the body of Christ. Without a period of formal or informal discipleship, a new Christian's growth may stagnate. Be available to gently guide others on their spiritual journey.

We may reach others like Dorcas did (Acts 9:36-42) by performing acts of service for fellow believers. Or we may minister to believers and unbelievers alike through acts of kindness. Barn raisings (complete with homemade meals). "Sewing circles," where women sew for the underprivileged. Clean-up and rebuilding projects after floods or other disasters. Even simple "cottage meetings" to cheer a confined neighbor. We can serve others in a variety of ways. Marvel at the miracles God will perform through you—if you are available.

In short, be alert to the opportunities that abound—to reach beyond.

But Why?

"Why aren't the results of our reaching out more positive?" one might ask.

First, because we are working with people. People will sometimes let us down and make poor decisions.

What people do with God is a personal choice. We cannot force them to serve Him, and neither will God.

Second, because *we* are people. We, too, will make mistakes. Although we have been given an awesome responsibility, we will blunder. At times we sin. We may even become competitive and jealous: "Our outreach is greater than yours." "We don't have as many resources as they do or we could do a better job." "I won't help at all if I can't . . ." How God must tire of our foolishness. "The fields are white to harvest, children, do not fight over the sickle," God would seem to say.

Third, the results are God's department, not ours. What may seem to be poor results can actually work together for good. How reassuring to know God can use even our mistakes to advance His kingdom. We are called to work faithfully but to leave the final results to God.

God calls His servants to reach beyond, even though there is risk involved.

Jack and Cindy were rewarded evil for good after many hours of serving a neighbor. While a third party was at fault, Jack and Cindy also found themselves in court, facing a judge who imposed a fine. Stung by the irony of it all, the couple and their family looked to God as their source of strength. Before a year had passed they could see how God really had used their circumstances to "work together for good."

"Help, help, help. All they want is help." Have you heard the complaint of Christians weary of helping people who seem to expect more and more financial help with little or no interest in spiritual help? Caution is in order. We don't want to fall into a web of helping people in ways that will support harmful addictions or facilitate sinful choices. If we find ourselves caught in such a trap we need to ask God for wisdom and discretion to set boundaries that will protect both the givers and the receivers from unprofitable assistance. I know of no blankets that cover all situations. We can begin a good work and pray for wisdom as we continue. It is not easy to learn to set boundaries or hold people accountable, but true helpers will do just that.

Everything considered, we still should not shrink from our Lord's commission to His followers: "But ye shall receive power, after that the Holy Ghost is come upon you: and ye shall be witnesses unto me both in Jerusalem, and in all Judaea, and in Samaria, and unto the uttermost part of the earth" (Acts 1:8).

Jerusalem and Judaea, Lord? You mean here around home — and in my community?

Yes, you can begin with the opportunities nearest you.

Even in Samaria, Lord? Even among the people we have scorned?

Yes, even there.

The uttermost parts of the earth, Lord, really? I am comfortable here.

But ye shall receive power, after that the Holy Ghost is come upon you: and ye shall be witnesses . . .

Scriptures

"But if our gospel be hid,
it is hid to them that are lost:
in whom the god of this world hath blinded

the minds of them which believe not,
lest the light of the glorious gospel of Christ,
who is the image of God, should shine unto them.

For we preach not ourselves,
but Christ Jesus the Lord;
and ourselves your servants for Jesus' sake.

For God, who commanded the light
to shine out of darkness,
hath shined in our hearts,
to give the light of the knowledge
of the glory of God
in the face of Jesus Christ.

But we have this treasure in earthen vessels,
that the excellency of the
power may be of God, and not of us."
2 Corinthians 4:3-7

"For whosoever shall call upon
the name of the Lord shall be saved.

How then shall they call on him
in whom they have not believed?
and how shall they believe
in him of whom they have not heard?
and how shall they hear without a preacher?

And how shall they preach,
except they be sent?
as it is written,
How beautiful are the feet of them
that preach the gospel of peace,
and bring glad tidings of good things!"
Romans 10:13-15

Prayer

Dear Lord and Saviour of Mankind,
  Forgive our foolish ways . . .
  We have not always recognized the importance of reaching beyond our worlds of comfort to preach the Gospel of peace and to bring glad tidings of good things. On occasions when we have reached out, we have fallen into traps, been rewarded evil for good, or been overly concerned about the results. Sometimes we have even stooped to competitiveness and jealousy — counting up stars in our crowns, as it were. How this must sadden You. Especially when You wish us to be busy with the harvest. What can I say, Dear God? We are earthen vessels. The substance we are asked to carry and share is — well, it is worth more than gold. Repair us and remake us, God. Conform us to the image of Your Son. He took upon Himself the form of a servant and was made in the likeness of men. He exchanged His throne for a manger. He ate with sinners and tax collectors. At the hands of the sinners He came to save He was tortured and killed, so that our sins could be forgiven by the merits of His blood. Oh, thank You, Jesus. Oh, God, how can we be silent?
  Forgive me for my failures. Fill me with Your Holy Ghost and with power. I want to pour the treasure from this earthen vessel in ways that the excellency of the power will be of You and not of me.

  Willing to Be Willing,

  _____

FOR HIS
GLORY!

CHAPTER 14

To the Praise of His Glory

I do not know when or where you will read this, but I want to personally invite you — fellow daughters of Eve, daughters of God — to join me on the bank of a wide stream, through the avenue of words.

Bare-limbed trees lace the horizon. A few have yet to share their colorful garment of leaves with the ground. The phoebes, whose simple songs summoned me from my garden so many seasons ago, have flown away again to sing in warmer backyards. This year's garden is all tucked in for a winter of rest, and I have come away to a favorite spot to worship the Lord and work on this last chapter. *How do I write a last chapter, Lord? What message of hope do I share with Your daughters?*

A brisk breeze nudges brown oak leaves at my feet. A few of them tumble into the stream beside me. They join the myriad of leaves that float past me, some dipping and turning in undercurrents, some floating lazily on the surface, and a few sitting upright with curved spines as if looking for a place to end their dizzying ride.

It occurs to me that the leaves are bound by their circumstances (not that they are capable of caring). Destined to change color and fall to the ground, they are unable to choose where they will land or what course they will take. Some will be stepped on or piled to be burned. Some will churn for miles in a stream. Others will "bed and breakfast" the forest floor.

Imagine the havoc that would result if leaves could insist on fair treatment and demand their own way. What if they stubbornly clung to the trees, demanding that God give them the landing site of their preference? Ridiculous thought, of course. But as I sit here watching some pitch and turn while others glide easily, I have to wonder if their lot in life compares a bit with our own.

We glide or churn through the seasons of life, tossed by circumstances, but not without a God who cares—and plans—and guides us in His will. Sometimes our circumstances clutch us in their grasp and we have to work hard to rise above them. As daughters of Eve we ask "Why?" But as daughters of God, we trust our Father, regardless of how we pitch and turn in the stream of life.

I know that some children's minds will churn with thoughts about empty housecoats, as mine did long ago. And while some children will experience hardships or deal with handicaps, others will grow up with relative ease. Some daughters of Eve will be blessed by husbands (or life in general), while others will be mocked or battered. A number of us will open well-stocked freezers today to prepare meat, vegetables, and fruit for ourselves or our families. Other sisters in Christ will search diligently for enough food to make a thin soup for hollow-eyed children. In countries blessed with freedoms, daughters of God will gather with other believers to openly worship God and drink in truths from His Word. In countries challenged by persecution, daughters of God will risk their lives to secretly gather in dimly-lit rooms while one precious Bible is read slowly so that those present may copy the gold of God's Word by hand.

None of us know when the tables may suddenly turn and those with abundance will taste of want, while those who have known great want will experience new freedoms.

What we do know is that God loves His children. Carefully, faithfully, omnisciently, He uses circumstances to bring about His will for our lives. God's will for all of His children is for their lives to bring glory to His holy name—in pleasant or unpleasant circumstances.

As daughters of Eve we find it difficult to always glorify God; our humanity and the weaknesses we inherited from Eve keep getting in our way. But as daughters of God we have been given a new nature. We have received power and strength beyond our own. Despite the circumstances or difficult situations of our lives, regardless of the way we are treated by other people, we really can live lives that bring glory to God.

To Praise His Glory

"That we should be to the praise of his glory, who first trusted in Christ" (Ephesians 1:12). *How does a daughter of God live to the praise of His glory?* I asked myself when the phrase caught my attention several years ago. The verses that precede verse 12 answered my question. Open your Bible and embrace the rich truths of Ephesians 1.

- God has blessed us with all spiritual blessings—in Christ (v. 3).

- He has chosen us to be holy and without blame before Him in love (v. 4).

- He decided beforehand to adopt us as children to Himself by Jesus Christ—according to the good pleasure of His will (v. 5).

- To the praise of the glory of His grace (by which He made us accepted in the beloved) (v. 6).

- We have redemption through His blood, and forgiveness of sins—according to the riches of His grace (v. 7).

- He really has abounded toward us (v. 8), making us to know the mystery of His will (v. 9) and gathering us together (v. 10) to our inheritance (v. 11).

Oh, to joy in the *riches of His grace*—we really can live to the praise of His glory—by His grace! Daughters of God can praise the *glory of His grace* through pleasant or difficult circumstances! (The writer in me knows to use only one exclamation point for the previous two sentences. The daughter in me wishes to add a string of them!!!!! Okay, I'll stop.)

Submerged in His Grace

Engrossed in watching the leaves and the stream, I see a turtle poke his head up from a submerged rock cavern. As I watch in wonder, his body glides through the water with ease and grace. With gentle strokes, he propels his heavy body over the rocks and then disappears into another watery cave. I have to wonder, is God giving me a simple illustration?

Lord, I am a lot like this turtle. On earth, my steps are awkward and slow. Sometimes my journey seems to be progressing with turtle speed. But today I have seen a turtle

228

swim, and I am filled with hope! When I am submerged in Your grace — when I am living in the joy of being a daughter of God — I can move forward with grace and beauty. Oh, THANK YOU, GOD! I really can live "to the praise of the glory of [Your] grace."

I left the streamside and returned home. (No, this wife and mother of five could not write a complete chapter in one sitting. My family needed me and my scribblings needed to be refined.)

Before I rewrote my rough draft, I met Margaret, a daughter of God who struggled with debilitating fears. "Sometimes I am afraid even to go outside, and my children get so afraid when I am full of fear," the young mother agonized. We talked and prayed about the circumstances that led to her fears. "You are making progress," I encouraged.

"Yes, I guess, but just little turtle steps."

I smiled. God was speaking again to two of His daughters. I could not resist.

"But have you ever seen a turtle *swim*?"

Writing this book has been a journey for me. And yes, sometimes it was torturous and slow. I learned more about my Father, God — His attention to detail, His goodness and sovereignty, His glorious outpouring of grace. When this last chapter is finished, I know what I will do. I will go to my closet and reach for the housecoat whose empty folds held the gift of a longing to know. I will pull back the plastic and feel the softness of flannel against my cheek. And I will thank God for His grace and the gifts He has given me — to teach me of His love for me, His daughter.

Dear Father,

My heart is overwhelmed with love and praise for You. I am humbled when I trace Your hand at work in my life. So many times You have used the things I have chafed at for my good and Your honor and glory. I can only praise the glory of Your grace!

Thank You for creating me as a daughter of Eve. Thank You for inviting me to be a daughter of God. Thank You for chastening me, cherishing me, and challenging me onward in my journey as Your daughter.

Gratefully Yours,
Your Daughter,

Brenda

Someday our lumbering steps as daughters of Eve will stop on the shores of the River Jordan. After crossing, we will pause just a moment to adorn ourselves in a wedding garment. The gates will open . . .

"Daughter, welcome home." When the words billow toward us, like the sound of many waters, will we quiver with anticipation? Reaching for the hand of the Bridegroom who gave His life to redeem us, we will be guided across the threshold of time into a glorious eternity.

"Come, ye blessed of my Father, inherit the kingdom prepared for you from the foundation of the world." What will it be like to meet Jesus face-to-face, hear His grand invitation, and follow the gesture of His nail-scarred hand toward the unmatched beauty of Heaven?

Our lives as daughters of Eve will fade into the glorious realities of our royal daughterhood. Never again will we doubt our position through Christ. The chastening will be over; the challenging onward, unnecessary; the cherishing will continue through eternity.

Finally and forever we will be perfected daughters of God!

Scriptures

"As the bridegroom rejoiceth over the bride,
so shall thy God rejoice over thee."
Isaiah 62:5

"But the God of all grace, who hath called
us unto his eternal glory by Christ Jesus,
after that ye have suffered a while,
make you perfect, stablish, strengthen, settle you.
To him be glory and dominion
for ever and ever. Amen."
1 Peter 5:10, 11

Prayer

Oh, my gracious, heavenly Father, my God,

How can I ever thank and praise You enough for the marvelous, miraculous invitation You have given to me? You have asked me to be part of the bride of Your dear Son. I, a dusty daughter of Eve, am invited to live by the glory of Your grace as a cherished daughter of God. I am so grateful to be —

Yours,

_____

Epilogue

The parts of my personal story and the stories of other women are included as a means of tethering the message to the everyday world of women readers. We are daughters of Eve, striving to live in victory as daughters of God. Names have been changed in some of the accounts. May God's name be praised as we mentor each other in our glorious daughterhood.

As I have given glimpses into my personal story, I wish to thank my family and friends for allowing me to depict details as I have remembered them. Thank you for willingly sharing parts of your lives for the benefit of others.

I want to honor my mother and the memory of my father. I can honestly say that "the lines are fallen unto me in pleasant places; yea, I have a goodly heritage" (Psalm 16:6). How thankful I am for what their lives have given to mine.

Since my father passed away, my mother has remarried, so I also owe gratitude to my stepfather—who happens to be the next-door grandparent of the young lady who approached me at my wash line in Chapter 12.

I want to especially thank my wonderful husband and children for allowing me to write. Thank you, John, LaNell, Lori, Eddie, Stan, and Holly for bearing with me through daughter-of-Eve moments while I wrote about the wonder of being a daughter of God.

May my Father's name be glorified!

Brenda (Furtak) Weaver

Endnotes

Chapter 1

1. "War—Liberia's Monster," in Christian Aid Ministries Newsletter, January 29, 2004, pp. 1, 4.

2. Read-A-Long Translation, *The Open Bible, Authorized King James Version* (Nashville: Thomas Nelson Publishers, 1975), p. 830.

Chapter 2

1. K. P. Yohannan, "Destined to Soar," in SEND! (Gospel for Asia News Magazine), Volume 24 (2004), p. 19.

2. Amy Carmichael, *Edges of His Ways* (Fort Washington, PA: CLC Publications, 1955, 2000 edition), p. 39.

Chapter 3

1. Joan Luckmann and Karen Sorensen, *Medical-Surgical Nursing* (Philadelphia: WB Saunders Co., 1974), p. 1307.

Chapter 4

1. Albert M. Wells, compiler, *Inspiring Quotations Contemporary and Classical* (Nashville: Thomas Nelson Publishers, 1988), pp. 192, 193, 206.

2. Elisabeth Elliot, *Passion and Purity* (Grand Rapids, Michigan: Fleming H. Revell, A Division of Baker Book House Co., 1984), pp. 80, 81.

Chapter 5

1. John and Barbara Coblentz, Audio tape set of *Faithful Women Seminar* (Plain City, Ohio: Deeper Life Ministries, November 2, 1996), Tape Number 3.

2. Ibid.

3. *The Open Bible Edition* of *The Holy Bible, KJV* (Nashville, TN: Thomas Nelson, Publishers, 1975), p. 1163.

4. John Coblentz Sr., sermon and study notes from writer's personal files, circa 1990.

Chapter 8
1. Wanda Wagler, Poem, "Marriage or Singlehood?" published by Christian Light Publications in *Companions,* January 7, 2001.

2. Lucy Martin, article, "Did you Miss the Boat?" published by Christian Light Publications in *Companions,* October 31, 1999.

Chapter 9
1. Henry Seidel Canby, ed., *Favorite Poems of Henry Wadsworth Longfellow* (Garden City, New York: Doubleday and Company, Inc., 1967), p. 183.

Chapter 10
1. Merna B. Shank, © 1983 (© 1984) Warner Press Inc., Anderson, Indiana. All rights reserved. Used by permission. (Reprinted from *My Soul's Delights* by Christian Light Publications, Harrisonburg, VA.).

2. Ibid, p. 13.

3. Carrie E. Breck, "Face to Face" (Song copyrighted 1927 by Grant C. Tullar), source: J. D. Brunk, S. F. Coffman, editors, *Church Hymnal* (Scottdale, PA: Mennonite Publishing House, 1927, renewal 1955), p. 107.

4. Taken from *Amazing Grace, 366 Inspiring Hymn Stories for Daily Devotions* complied by Kenneth W. Osbeck. Published by Kregel Publications, Grand Rapids, MI. Used by permission of the publisher. All rights reserved.

Chapter 11

1. Monica Miller, poem from writer's personal files, used by permission, circa 1989.

Christian Light Publications, Inc., is a nonprofit, conservative Mennonite publishing company providing Christ-centered, Biblical literature including books, Gospel tracts, Sunday school materials, summer Bible school materials, and a full curriculum for Christian day schools and homeschools. Though produced primarily in English, some books, tracts, and school materials are also available in Spanish.

For more information about the ministry of CLP or its publications, or for spiritual help, please contact us at:

Christian Light Publications, Inc.
P. O. Box 1212
Harrisonburg, VA 22803-1212

Telephone—540-434-0768
Fax—540-433-8896
E-mail—info@clp.org
www.clp.org